PENGUIN BOOKS

Writing for Children

Eleanor Nilsson is a well-known and highly regarded writer for children who has had a wide variety of books published for both younger and older readers.

Born in Stirling, Scotland, Eleanor now teaches courses in children's literature and the writing of children's books at the University of South Australia. Her first book, *Parrot Fashion*, was published in 1983, and more recently *The Black Duck* was shortlisted for the 1991 Australian Children's Book of the Year Award for Younger Readers. Her latest book, *The House Guest*, for older readers, won the National Children's Book Award in the 1992 Adelaide Festival Awards for Literature and also won the 1992 Australian Children's Book of the Year Award for Older Readers. It has also been shortlisted for the 1992 Victorian Premier's Literary Award (Children's Books).

Eleanor lives in Coromandel Valley with her husband Neil and her son Martin. Her daughter Catherine now lives in Perth where she is studying to be a vet.

By the same author

Eleanor Nilsson

Writing for Children

Penguin Books

Penguin Books Australia Ltd
487 Maroondah Highway, PO Box 257
Ringwood, Victoria 3134, Australia
Penguin Books Ltd
Harmondsworth, Middlesex, England
Viking Penguin, A Division of Penguin Books USA Inc.
375 Hudson Street, New York, New York 10014, USA
Penguin Books Canada Limited
10 Alcorn Avenue, Toronto, Ontario, Canada M4V 3B2
Penguin Books (N.Z.) Ltd
182-190 Wairau Road, Auckland 10, New Zealand

First published by Penguin Books Australia, 1992
1 3 5 7 9 10 8 6 4 2
Copyright © Eleanor Nilsson, 1992

Typeset in 12 pt Bembo by Midland Typesetters, Maryborough, Vic.
Made and printed in Australia by Australian Print Group, Maryborough, Vic.

National Library of Australia
Cataloguing-in-Publication data:

Nilsson, Eleanor, 1939–
Writing for children.

ISBN 0 14 013352 6.

1. Children's literature—Authorship. 2. Children's literature—
Technique. I. Title.

808.068

To Helen
and
in memory of my father,
Murdoch Luke

I would like to thank George and Beryl Siemionow of *Bees Knees Books*, Blackwood, for their suggestions and help with titles.

Contents

CONTENTS

CHAPTER 3

Picture Books

Length. You have to want to turn the page. Characterisation. Ideas. A concentrated style. Repetition. Reading your work aloud. Titles. Story-telling. Visualising. Drafts. Rhymed picture books.
Try this!

CHAPTER 4

Story Books (6–10 years)

Basic considerations. Ideas. Point of view. Characterisation. Plot: how to develop your ideas. Language.
Try this!

CHAPTER 5

Novels and Short Stories (11+ years): The Organisation of Your Story

Making a start. Models. Beginnings. Developing your story. Endings.
Try this!

CONTENTS

CHAPTER 6

**Novels and Short Stories (11+ years):
Further Aspects of Technique**
Characterisation. Settings. Dialogue. Point of view.
Chapter endings. Making your writing convincing.
Fantasy and science fiction.
Try this!
119

CHAPTER 7

Editing Your Own Work
Getting started. General polishing. Punctuation.
Is your story logical? Salvaging. Expansions.
Little tips.
Try this!
155

CHAPTER 8

Marketing Your Manuscript
Can I get something published? Have I got my
manuscript into the best possible shape? Giving your
manuscript the best possible chance. Sending your
manuscript off. Editorial help. The publisher's reader.
Sharing your joy. An emotional business.
183

Bibliography
205

CHAPTER 1

Writing for Children

Many people think at some stage that they would like to write for children, but feel that it is an impossible task. They don't know anything about writing, and worse still, they often feel that they don't know very much about children. Let's tackle the second difficulty first. I believe that it isn't really a difficulty at all, and suggests a false approach to the whole subject.

CHILDREN

It is common for children's writers to claim that they don't really write for children. And this is often considered to be a very strange response indeed – but is it? They will say, for example, that they write for themselves, or 'for their story'. Arthur Ransome, author of the famous *Swallows and Amazons* series, said: 'You write not *for* children but for yourself, and if, by good fortune, children enjoy what you enjoy, why then you are a writer of children's books . . .' C. S. Lewis quoted the extreme example of Arthur Mee who is claimed to have said that he'd 'never met a child and never wished to; it was, from his point of view, a bit of luck that boys liked reading what he liked writing.' And the very popular children's author Joan Aiken had this to say in an article she wrote for *Reading Time*: 'When I write I am not thinking about the reader; the story is coming out of me under its own power.'

All this shouldn't really surprise us: we don't expect the writer of adult fiction (but note that we usually do not use the adjective 'adult', unless we are referring to something pornographic) to keep the reader in mind throughout. No more, I believe, should we expect this of the children's writer. At this point the fear of children's writers makes itself felt: maybe there is something childish about them, if they write to please themselves and what they then complete is published for children. Leon Garfield voices this fear, humorously, in an article in Edward Blishen's *The Thorny Paradise*: 'A certain shame creeps in that our deepest thoughts make common ground with conkers and model aeroplanes.'

But Garfield's 'conkers' and 'model aeroplanes' do suggest a clue. Writing for children is primarily a question of subject matter and point of view. If you want to write a story about a child's love for a horse or about a wombat's fear of the dark, then it seems almost certain that it is a children's story you are considering. Many children's stories are about children or about animals or about the relationships between them, and if you want to tell your story from the *point of view* of the children or the animal, then it is practically certain that you are thinking of a children's story. It is always possible to think of exceptions, of course, like Richard Adams's *Watership Down* perhaps (about animals but

in many ways more suited to an adult readership) or
A High Wind in Jamaica by Richard Hughes; but in most
cases it will be a children's story that you have in mind.
The age of the child very often determines the age
audience the publisher will aim at in packaging the
book. Generally publishers believe that children like to
read about children slightly older than themselves, so
that a book intended to reach an audience of eleven or
twelve-year-olds might well have as its main character a
child of thirteen or fourteen. By the way, I am using
'point of view' in the technical sense, not to mean
anything to do with opinion, but rather the stance from
which a story is told: through which particular character
or characters the story is actually being filtered.

Nina Bawden, who writes popular fiction for adults
as well as novels for children, says that to her the whole
question of what constitutes a children's book resolves
itself into this matter of point of view. Here is how she
puts it in an article called 'A Dead Pig and My Father'.
She describes the very different reactions which she and
her mother had to the sight of her father's ship coming in,
while a bloated dead pig bobbed past them in the water.

*We were both there together, caught up in the same, highly charged
emotional situation, but we each saw it quite differently. And the
important difference between writing for adults and writing for
children is not style or subject matter, though those things come
into it, but the point of view you're looking from . . . There you
have it. My secret is out, as they say. As far as I am concerned,
the only real difference between writing for adults or for children is
whose eyes I am looking through. My mother's – standing on
Tilbury Docks and wishing her wretched child would smile and be
nice. Or the little girl's, standing beside her and watching a dead
pig in the water, instead of her father's ship coming in.*

Style does, of course, come into it also. Henry James's *What Maisie Knew* has the viewpoint of a child at its centre, but the style is so intricate and the perceptions so fine that it would be too difficult for most children (and perhaps for many adults) to comprehend.

Indeed style is crucial in children's writing. It is so important, especially in the case of younger children, to put what you have to say simply, without appearing in any way to be talking down to your audience. Often, when you do become aware of audience in a piece of writing for children it is because there is something wrong with it: there is that dreadful sense of patronage, of condescension, which it should be the author's main task to avoid.

That is why, in a sense, it is much safer to write for yourself, because you will then try to write something that you are pleased with. A better way of saying it might be that you should write for your story, be true to your story, rather than to some hypothetical audience out there. And every story seems to dictate its own style. You will see what I mean when you start writing.

It has never been proved that children's responses to their reading are different in kind from those of adults. Educational writers often talk at length about the ways in which children's books should differ from adults', but these are often in superficial matters such as length, size of print and so on. As Phyllis Whitney reminds us in her book *Writing Juvenile Stories and Novels*, if you consider the fact that the stories which we best remember, both as adults and as children, are the ones which moved us emotionally, you are ready to appreciate that as readers, both children and adults are looking for much the same things, and are responding in much the same way. Children are not a different race: they respond emotionally in the same way we do to stories. Phyllis Whitney goes on to say:

There is a universality about human needs, no matter what the age or position of the people involved. When you understand that, there will be no danger of your writing down to the readers, and your stories will take on a warmth that will make your readers respond with genuine feeling.

If you listen to the writers of children's books you get the same sense of the similarity of audience. A writer like Jane Gardam, who writes books which are marketed for all age categories of readers, believes that there is 'no difference' in her approach to writing for children and for adults. And C. S. Lewis, in his famous essay 'On Three Ways of Writing for Children', says:

I put in what I would have liked to read when I was a child and what I still like reading now that I am in my fifties. And in the same essay: *I am almost inclined to set it up as a canon that a children's story which is enjoyed only by children is a bad children's story.*

I don't believe then that it is necessary to rush off and try out your story on a young audience. Even if you do, and the children next door love it, it does not necessarily mean that a publisher will be interested in it.

If you have no contact with young children at all, I wouldn't worry about it: it is still perfectly possible to write children's stories. After all, you have been a child yourself. You have had contact with children through-out your life. You see them on buses, coming out of school, you watch films about them, you read about them in the newspaper. You will find that much of what you write about will be based on your own experiences, present and past.

WRITING

And now to look at the writing part of it. Writing fiction appears to be quite a common ambition, but we all seem to be overcome with terror at the thought of it. Everyone speaks of writing one day, 'One day when I get the time'. Or people will say, 'I would like to write, but I'm not a creative person'. This may just be a way out, of course, but if you genuinely want to write, it is a shame if you think that the whole process has got something to do with inspiration. I'm afraid that writing has got far more to do with hard work than with anything else. The person who manages one day to sit down and write a brilliant story in ten days is someone who has had a lot of practice. You wouldn't expect to go out to the shed and make a beautifully proportioned table without having spent many hours learning the necessary skills. It is the same with writing. Writing is simply a matter of picking up skills through practice and through detailed observation of what other, more experienced writers do.

Phyllis Whitney once attended a writers' seminar where the woman next to her said of the first speaker: 'She still hasn't told us her secret, has she?' The only secret there is, says Whitney, is that you must want to do it enough.

Writing is very hard work. It needs a lot of concentration, and it is always much easier to do something else: water the garden, wash the car, return a book to a friend, go out to lunch. We can always put other activities in front of it if we wish. It also takes a lot of time, but as Phyllis Whitney puts it:

Time is not something you "have". It is not even something you "find". It is something you make. *You make it forcibly by pushing other things out of the way. Other things you want to do; even other things you ought to do.*

It can be quite humiliating too when you start, in that all your life you have been reading stories and now you find that you are not exactly sure what a story is.

One way to get started is to think about what stories you liked reading as a child. It is very likely that you will want to write that kind of a story yourself. For years I was haunted by a story, without knowing its source, where a child was late for school because on his way there he found a rabbit either dead or dying by the side of the road. I remembered him standing, disgraced in the schoolroom because he was so late, and then, with the marks of tears on his face, opening his jacket and showing the sad bundle there. I remember another story about a toy shop and one about a dog called Scamp. The last two were books that I owned. The first, I learned only recently, was a story that my brother had asked my mother to read to us over and over again when we were young children, and hence the vivid memory. Clearly, I did tend to like 'weepy' stories as a child, and perhaps (to some extent, anyway) I write them now. Jot down what you can remember of your early reading: it may help you in your quest for a story.

IDEAS

The main problem, when people want to write, is finding the ideas. 'I'd really like to write,' someone will say, 'but I never seem to get any ideas.' And so the writing task is postponed until those elusive ideas turn up. But if you wait till you get a really good idea before you start to write you will wait for ever. When you get to sixty or seventy or thirty or whatever you yourself see as the cut-off point for this ambition, you will say, with a sigh, 'Oh well, obviously I'm not a writer. I'm not a creative person.'

Now it seems to me that each one of us *is* a creative person – we just have to give ourselves the chance. There is no point in waiting for inspiration to descend from on high. Writing isn't like that. The way to get ideas is to start writing. Try to write for a little while every day, even if it is only for ten minutes. Everyone can find ten minutes in a day to do what they really want to do. Each day just sit at your desk at the same time for ten minutes. You don't need to try to write a story: pamper yourself. Remember that you are a beginning writer and that you can't expect to be producing tables straight away. Go for breadboards. Write about anything: a conversation you overheard at the school gate, what someone said at the butcher's, an incident you remember from your childhood, what you've noticed has been happening in your garden over the last week, what you can see and hear out of your window as you write, what you can't stand about your best friend. *Anything*, just so long as it gets you writing.

You will find that you are rusty, that the words just won't behave in the ways that they should, that you can't say exactly what you mean. That's to be expected:

fluency and accuracy are all a matter of practice. You will have to get your tools in order (that is, your words) before you can expect to write the stories that we all have in us somewhere, eager and anxious to come out.

Steady, dedicated writing practice like this (just like playing scales on the piano) pays off in all sorts of areas. Letter-writing becomes much easier, for example. It also becomes easier to say exactly what you mean. Mind you, I think there is an occupational hazard in all this: as a writer you will tend to say what you mean in conversation too. You may find that it is not easy to cloak or hide how you feel about things because on paper you have been trying to get rid of the barrier that comes between you and what you really want to say.

ENCOURAGING YOURSELF TO WRITE

In the early stages, before you get encouraged by praise from the outside in the form of publication, it is very important that you consciously supply yourself with the conditions that will help you to write. Some of these are physical, some psychological. Make sure you have a pleasant place to write in, for example. Find a room in the house and make it your own, so that your desk can be permanently set up with your working materials. If you can't find a whole room, then set up a corner of a quiet one with a desk and adequate lighting for day or night work.

And what about (although this may seem frivolous) getting dressed up to write? Keats, after all, always wore a clean shirt for composition. Mind you, as someone once remarked, he probably didn't have to launder it first.

Find out what is the best time of day for you to write, assuming that you do have a choice of times. Maybe you can set yourself up at 9 am when you are still fresh. Most people find that they have a time in the day when they are at their freshest and most optimistic. Some established writers work from 9 to 11 or 12 every day; others, like Elizabeth Jolley, work only at nights. Others again, like P. D. James (the famous detective story writer) had to get up at 4 am when she started writing, because she had a full-time job in the public service, an invalid husband and teenage daughters, and there was no other quiet time possible. Find your best time and stick to it. You will soon discover that you will look forward to your quiet time tucked away with your equipment and your words. You'll then want to sit for more than ten minutes, and the 'pocket of time', as Joan Aiken calls the time that we can find if we really want to, will start to stretch.

Speaking of equipment, you really do need to be able to produce typewritten copy. Handwritten work, if your handwriting is anything like mine, becomes too hard to read later when you are no longer quite so familiar with your story. In these days too when there are many writers and much competition, when piles of manuscripts decorate the floors and desks of publishing houses, you really can't expect an exhausted, overworked editor to be excited about reading a handwritten manuscript. (Handwritten work doesn't photocopy well either – and remember that you should always keep at least one copy of your story for yourself.)

I think there is a kind of folklore about writing by hand. Some people seem to believe that no one can do anything truly creative unless it comes out, at least initially, in a handwritten form. Perhaps they see the difference between doing this and putting work straight onto the typewriter or word processor as the difference between hand-woven and machine-made carpets. But really this is just romance. And as I have said above, it isn't helpful to look at writing in terms of creativity anyway, and the best tools now available for your work are the word processing programs on computers. Do we really believe that Tolstoy would have written *War and Peace* by hand if he could have bought a Macintosh or an IBM? It does remain true, however, that some people, including established writers like Elizabeth Jolley, are often more comfortable writing in longhand first. We all just have to work out the method that suits us best. Still, if you can get used to composing on the screen it will save you a lot of time.

The price of technology keeps coming down, and the price of typewriters and computers is actually less every year. If you can, pamper yourself and buy a computer; for stories (as we know) do not descend in a finished form from above, but need continual working and reworking. Even once you get your story accepted by a publisher, it is likely that you will be asked to make quite a few changes to it. It is so easy to alter material on the computer screen: you can add bits and take away bits without tedious retyping. You can change the page numbers all the way through a longer manuscript if you decide to add a chapter, and so on. Surround yourself with the best equipment you can afford, even to the details: soft rubbers, sharp clear pencils, a firm straight ruler.

Writing tends to be a fairly emotional business, even for people whom you might consider to be successful. It is perhaps even more emotional when we are starting out. It is very important to have someone that you can talk to about your writing. It may be someone in the family, in which case you are lucky, for it is someone on hand whom you can consult at any time. Writing is often such a lonely, difficult business that many people give up, I am sure, because they do not get encouragement at the right time. Of course you will have to expect criticism as well; we're not always the best judges of what we write, especially at the beginning, and are likely to feel thrilled the first time we produce something that is recognisably a story. But we can't expect even a sympathetic audience to jump up and down with delight at our early attempts.

Perhaps this is one of the hardest things to get used to as a writer: to take, and at times accept, criticism of a story whether it is from a friend, a publisher's reader, or an editor. Of course it is possible that your friend is wrong in his or her criticism; it is even possible that the reader or the editor is wrong. But you have to remember that the people in these latter two categories are very experienced, and you will at least have to consider the criticism, and look at it as coolly and rationally as you can. You must learn to distance yourself from your story. Pretend that someone else has written it, if you can. This is easier if you finish a story and put it away for a week or two or even a month, rather than rushing straight off to the post office with it. Remember, you have to be the first reader and the first critic of what you write.

But to get back to the 'coolly' and 'rationally'. Unfortunately there is very little that is cool or rational about the budding writer. Often publishers and friends don't understand why a writer gets so upset when all they want to do is to help him (or her) to produce a better story – and after all, the writer has *asked* for help, they may think indignantly. But it becomes easier for them to understand if they realise that you, the writer, have made the story out of nothing – you have created it. It's as if someone criticised one of your children, especially if you have just finished working on it. The story a writer is working on at the time is closest to his or her heart. We all learn to be more dispassionate about earlier stories.

It's more than that too, though. You will find, to your amazement, that when you write stories they provide a map of your mind. The stories will tell you what your secret fears are: secret even to yourself, I mean. They will show you what you are most interested in, and what experiences have had the most effect on you. So, you didn't realise that you hadn't got over your parents splitting up when you were nine; you will find the experiences that are still very important to you will keep cropping up in your stories. Anything that you still feel deeply about, even if unconsciously, is sure to surface, even if it is in a disguised form.

So *this* is really why we feel so sensitive about our stories. Even when they are supposedly written for very young children, they are providing a coding of what is most important to us. This is true, anyway, when we are writing honestly for children. If we are just writing something that doesn't engage our feelings or interests or memories at all, something that somehow we feel will *do* for children, we may get it published, but it won't be worth publishing.

Discipline yourself so that you can always write, otherwise other tasks will seem easier very often and you will soon drift off to them. It seems to me that what we can produce on paper or on the screen when we don't feel like it, isn't likely to be terribly different in quality from what we can produce when we do. The very successful writer for children and for adults, Roald Dahl, claims that he gets all his ideas at the typewriter. And I don't suppose that he always feels like sitting there. First we start writing, *then* we get the ideas. That is the most important piece of advice I or anyone else can give you about writing. We learn to write by writing, not by thinking about writing. We also learn to write by imitating other authors.

If you really can't overcome your resistance to writing on any one day, do something related. Study suspense techniques and plotting in the detective stories of P. D. James, Ruth Rendell or Agatha Christie, for example. Study characterisation in E. B. White's *Charlotte's Web* or Ivan Southall's *Josh* or in George Eliot's *Middlemarch*. Look at how Jane Austen distinguishes her characters through their distinctive syntax and word choice. We don't need to restrict ourselves to children's writers to get help. Remember, the world is full of people who mean to write 'one day': people who are waiting for either the time or the inspiration or both. But the way to get inspiration is to sit at your desk – and write.

TRY THIS!

- Describe the conditions, physical and psychological, under which you write.

- Which stories do you remember from your own childhood? Do they seem to have common elements?

- Write two paragraphs on anything that has captured your interest in the last week.

CHAPTER 2

Marketable Categories of Children's Books

It is a good idea to get clear in your mind the kinds of books marketed for children. Publishers *do* think in terms of the age of the child being catered for, even if many writers don't; and, on the face of it at least, books tend to be marketed for children of different age ranges.

Fiction for children can be divided up roughly into the following categories:

picture books
story books (6–10 years)
full-length novels (11+ years through to adolescence)

PICTURE BOOK TEXTS

Many different kinds of book are subsumed under the category of picture book, and the texts for these vary greatly in length from as little as one sentence for the whole book (as in *Rosie's Walk* by Pat Hutchins, for example) to as many as 2000 words or more. At the upper word limits it is possible for the same text to be marketed either as a picture book or as a book for younger readers. I suppose this decision must depend on how well the publisher thinks the text would illustrate. Will it improve the book to illustrate the text or is the text so detailed and visual in its own right that only an occasional background illustration is warranted?

In Australia the picture book texts which seem to have won most acclaim in book awards have been the short ones, those of 300 to 800 words approximately. *John Brown, Rose and the Midnight Cat, The Friends of Emily Culpepper, Possum Magic*, and more recently, *Felix and Alexander* and *The Very Best of Friends* have all been about this length. Certainly the overall design of a book will then tend to look better: the text can be spaced out in a more even and symmetrical manner from page to page, and the larger amounts of white space on each page create a cleaner, a tidier effect. It is harder to position a longer text in as aesthetic a way, and to get the same balance of text to picture in each double spread. Where the text is substantially longer, the person designing the book often keeps the words on one side of each double spread, and the pictures on the other. *Whistle up the Chimney* by Nan Hunt and illustrated by Craig Smith has this sort of format, as has *The Prowler* with the same illustrator and with the text by Geoffrey Dutton. There are no rules about this, of course: Terry Denton's *Felix and Alexander*, for example, is a short text, but the words appear on only one side of the page, while Graham Oakley's *Henry's Quest* is a long text positioned on both sides. So much will depend on how the publisher, designer and editor see the text and the illustrations as working together.

STORY BOOKS (6–10 YEARS)

This is an area which keeps changing all the time. Once this section would have been referred to as 'Junior Fiction', at the time when, in Australia, the Children's Book Council brought in a new category in its prizes called the Junior Book of the Year Award. Christobel Mattingley and Patricia Mullins won the award in its first year (1982) with *Rummage* (2650 words), and Robin Klein and Alison Lester in its second with *Thing* (about 3500 words). Both these books are really picture books with extended texts. Now the award is simply called 'Book of the Year: Younger Readers', and has been given to progressively longer and longer illustrated story books. Jennifer Rowe, the editor of the *Australian Women's Weekly* and former chief editor at Angus & Robertson, has been winning this award (writing as Emily Rodda) since 1985 in every alternate year: with *Something Special* (1985), *Pigs Might Fly* (1987), *The Best-kept Secret* (1989) and *Finders Keepers* (1991).

Some books within this range are particularly useful for reading aloud to children before they can read for themselves, but they may also be used as story books for older children. Books which read well aloud tend to be those whose language has a rhythmic, poetic quality, like Rudyard Kipling's *Just So Stories* and A. A. Milne's *Winnie-the-Pooh*. More recent examples are Rumer Godden's *The Mousewife*, Russell Hoban's *Dinner at Alberta's* and Ted Hughes's *How the Whale Became and Other Stories*.

Publishers are now bringing out series especially for this age group. A particularly attractive one, with quality books in it, including three by Jane Gardam and two by Bernard Ashley, is the Julia MacRae Blackbird

Series. The books have hard, laminated covers in full colour, large clear print that looks like ordinary typing because the right-hand margin is not justified, and black-and-white illustrations throughout the texts. These vary in length from about 3000 to 6000 words, but the books are all kept to 44 pages by varying the number and positioning of the illustrations.

Another prestigious series is the Young Puffin range, whose titles are taken from all over the publishing world. These are paperback books with bright, attractive covers, the print size depending on the intended age group. Indeed the size of print is a very good guide for determining what age range the publishers have in mind for a book. Bernard Ashley's *Dinner Ladies Don't Count* and Jane Gardam's *Bridget and William* translated into Puffin format are in very large print and are intended for the youngest age range within this form. Jan Mark's *The Dead Letter Box*, in slightly smaller print and running at about 8000 words, is clearly considered to be more demanding.

One effect of the large print is to make books appear longer than they actually are. What is virtually only a short story appears in novel form. This not only helps with the marketing of a book: it makes reading a very positive experience early for children, for the large print and the copious illustrations ensure that they can turn over the pages quickly. They also have the satisfaction of feeling that they have read a whole book.

Stories can be as simple as Jean Kenward's *Ragdolly Anna* or as difficult as a book like Nina Warner Hooke's *The Snow Kitten*. In between are titles like Christobel Mattingley's carefully ordered *Duck Boy* or Emily Rodda's appealing fantasies, such as *Pigs Might Fly* and *The Best-kept Secret*. This is an area of the market which has been booming in recent years, and I think it is true to say that you are more likely to be successful in getting something published within this area. There are many, many excellent authors who write for the next level of difficulty, the full-length novel, but there seems to be plenty of room still for competent writers for younger children.

FULL-LENGTH NOVELS

Younger age group (11+ years)

This category includes many fine and sophisticated texts; there is very little restriction here to constrain the eager writer. Texts vary in length from about 18,000 words (the size of Gillian Rubinstein's *Answers to Brute*) to 60,000 words (the length of *Space Demons*, also by Gillian Rubinstein). There is therefore plenty of room to develop your idea and few constraints in the way in so far as sentence structure and word choice are concerned. You may even, if you wish, interweave two stories, as happens in *Space Demons* with the alternating points of view of Andrew and Elaine.

Many twentieth century classics for children fit into this classification – from works early in the century like Edith Nesbit's *Five Children and It* and Frances Hodgson Burnett's *The Secret Garden* to classics of the fifties like Philippa Pearce's *Tom's Midnight Garden*, Lucy Boston's *The Children of Green Knowe* and Mary Norton's *The Borrowers*. There is no lack of excellent models here.

In Australia many of our best authors write for the 11+ age group – not only more recent writers like Robin

Klein and Gillian Rubinstein, but older, well established authors like Joan Phipson with her thriller *The Cats*, Ivan Southall with *Bread and Honey*, Patricia Wrightson with *A Little Fear* and Eleanor Spence with her sensitive *A Candle for Saint Antony*.

Adolescent fiction

There is considerable variety in length and difficulty and indeed in quality within this area, in which the distinguishing feature often is that stories are about the lives of teenagers or young adults. There is really no compelling reason why the competent reader cannot now go straight on to adult fiction, but it has been felt in recent years that books which feature adolescents will be more appealing (or 'relevant') to this age group and will keep young people reading. These books tend to focus on problems; not that all books don't do this, but the intention seems to be more explicit here. Length tends to be shorter than for adult fiction; indeed books are often hardly longer than for the 11+ age group and may indeed be shorter. Within this area there are easier options with larger print: options like the *Sweet Dreams* series – intended for teenage girls interested in romances.

There are also difficult but more rewarding books which are marketed as teenage fiction only because they have an adolescent as a protagonist: books published in England like Jane Gardam's *The Summer After the Funeral*, Alan Garner's *Red Shift*, William Mayne's *The Jersey Shore* and Janni Howker's *Badger on the Barge*; and in Australia like Isobelle Carmody's *The Farseekers*, Gary Crew's *Strange Objects* and Victor Kelleher's *Taronga*. I believe that quality adolescent fiction is more likely to come from books that are *about* adolescents rather than books that are *for* adolescents in the sense that they concentrate too narrowly on the expectations (or the alleged 'needs') of their likely audience.

It is interesting to note just how much of the material coming out for adolescents in Australia in recent years is science fiction or fantasy. Early books with this orientation were Lee Harding's *Displaced Person* (published in 1979) and his later novel *Waiting for the End of the World*. Since then we have had a whole range of writing in these areas: Gillian Rubinstein's award-winning *Beyond the Labyrinth*, the first two volumes of Isobelle Carmody's trilogy *Obernewtyn* and *The Farseekers*, Caroline Macdonald's *The Lake at the End of the World* and *The Eye Witness*, and many Kelleher titles including *Brother Night* and *Master of the Grove*. If you are familiar with fantasy and science fiction you will already be aware that, far from being a kind of retreat from contemporary problems, these forms very often provide the most effective way of dealing with them.

This is a time of rich experimentation in the Australian children's novel as you will realise if you consider some of the books which have come out just in the last few years. Gillian Rubinstein uses the present tense and optional endings in *Beyond the Labyrinth*. Victor Kelleher makes use of different modes of fiction in *Del-Del* where the reader is invited to choose between realistic, fantasy or science fiction explanations of the small boy Sam's frightening behaviour. Caroline Macdonald employs double or multiple viewpoints in *The Lake at the End of the World* and *The Eye Witness* respectively. In *Strange Objects* Gary Crew presents, in the form of 'documents', material (past and present) about the wreck of the *Batavia*. This has the effect of giving the material the appearance of a history and yet there is a rich element of fantasy within this novel too.

You may find it useful to refer to Agnes Nieuwenhuizen's book about contemporary Australian adolescent fiction. It is called *No Kidding* (published in 1991 by Pan Macmillan) and is based on interviews with twelve Australian authors.

Now might be the time to familiarise yourself with all the marketable categories of children's books by reading selected titles within each section. This might help to alert you early to the area which will finally appeal to you the most. Of course some writers like Jane Gardam, Jan Mark, William Mayne, Robin Klein and Gillian Rubinstein manage to write in all or most of the categories, so you needn't feel you have to limit yourself to one.

The chapters which follow will look in detail at the different categories and will alert you to various short cuts in learning the trade. If you have already been submitting to publishers without success it may be because your work has been cutting across the categories: you may have been writing something of 30,000 words but with material too young for a child who could handle the length; or alternatively, you may have been writing at 10,000 words with material that is suitable only for adolescents. The main thing is to believe that the skills involved in writing for children are learnable and to remember that *you have to want to do it enough*.

TRY THIS!

- What marketable category of children's story would you most like to write and why? Give a short description of a book in this category which you admire.

- What do you consider are your main strengths and weaknesses as a writer at the moment?

- We looked briefly at experimentation in the modern Australian children's novel. Can you think of any other techniques which might successfully be adapted from the adult novel to the children's?

CHAPTER 3

Picture Books

The beginning writer tends to be attracted to the picture book area, and it is certainly true that many children's writers have begun their careers with a picture book text. Robin Klein is a notable example. But, beware! Although short (and writing at length is rather terrifying for most people when starting out) the picture book text is a highly sophisticated and difficult form of writing. It embodies its own kind of diction, it incorporates the very essence of the story form, and the writer has to be prepared to adapt his or her text to the requirements of the publisher's design department and the illustrator. A lot of heartache frequently lies behind these beautifully finished, full-colour productions. At the same time if you do succeed in having a text published, you will find it very exciting and rewarding to see your idea presented in this way.

You can save quite a lot of time that you might otherwise spend in writing stories that do not really fit this category, by thinking about some of its characteristics.

LENGTH

A picture book has thirty-two pages, nearly always. This means that you should think of your story (allowing room for the title page and so on) in terms of fourteen or fifteen paragraphs, whether the paragraph is to be positioned on one side of each double spread, or divided over it. It is even a good idea to put these paragraphs, as you write them, on separate pages, to remind yourself of where a page would turn over. Which brings me to the stern edict of every publisher of picture books, or indeed of any book:

YOU HAVE TO WANT TO TURN THE PAGE

It doesn't matter how beautifully you write, or how excellently your characters are defined, your publisher will tell you that if your reader isn't going to want to read on, all the rest is worthless. You must be able to interest your reader in your story. Fortunately, these story-telling skills can be learnt.

Where a text is as short as a picture book one is, the positioning of every word is crucial. You have to try to create suspense, the desire to read on, and with so few words. Actually, however, you can use the form of the picture book to your advantage for this. *The Story About Ping*, published in 1935 and still a favourite with children, can be used as a model. Note how Marjorie Flack divides up her sentences to achieve this effect:

But down came (p. 23)
*a basket all over Ping and he could see no more of the Boy or the
boat or the sky or the beautiful yellow water of the Yangtze river.*
(p. 24)

But up (p. 29)
*marched Ping, up over the little bridge and SPANK
came the cane on Ping's back!* (pp. 30-31)

You can see the anticipation that is aroused by this
very simple device.

Maurice Sendak's famous picture book, *Where the Wild
Things Are*, ends with this sentence, spread over four
pages. Notice what he keeps for the last page:

*The wild things roared their terrible roars and gnashed their
terrible teeth and rolled their terrible eyes and showed their
terrible claws but Max stepped into his private boat and waved
good-bye*

*and sailed back over a year
and in and out of weeks
and through a day*

*and into the night of his very own room
where he found his supper waiting for him*

and it was still hot.

Of course, this is not the only way in which you can
achieve suspense – by the positioning of words. You can
arouse concern for a character by placing him or her in
an unpleasant or dangerous position. Stories which do
this move from a situation of danger or misery of some

kind, to a resolution of comparative calm. A character will overcome a fear, like the child in *There's a Sea in My Bedroom*; Hush manages to become visible again in *Possum Magic*; the bear believes that he has been recognised again as a bear in *The Bear Who Wanted to Stay a Bear*; in *The Very Best of Friends* Jessie manages to accept what has happened to her and appreciate what she has been left with, and Felix and Alexander, in the picture book of that name, find their way home.

CHARACTERISATION

It seems sensible, since you have so few words to play with in a picture book text, to keep your characterisation down as much as possible. You may find that one, or at most two main characters, where the story is about some shift in their relationship perhaps, will be all that you need. *The Story About Ping* is just that. *Willy the Wimp* is about Willy, and *The Friends of Emily Culpepper*, in spite of the title, is about Emily. *John Brown, Rose and the Midnight Cat*, with a deservedly famous (Australian) text by Jenny Wagner, is about a shift in the relationship between John Brown and Rose. Similarly, the winner of the 1990 Australian Picture Book of the Year Award, *The Very Best of Friends*, (text by Margaret Wild and illustrated by Julie Vivas) focuses on a change in the relationship between Jessie and the cat William. Your reader needs to become concerned about the fate of your character or characters, and since space is limited, you are more likely to achieve this by concentrating on one or two.

It is interesting to note that although most *story* books

for children centre on a child, many *picture* books have adults as their focus or at least as one of their main characters. Emily Culpepper, Rose and Jessie are in central focus in the picture books named above, as is the grandmother in Margaret Wild's touching story about memory loss: *Remember Me*.

IDEAS

Although picture books are purportedly for the youngest age group, their authors often deal with quite sophisticated, or at least fundamental, ideas. You might say, if you had to, because it always sounds diminishing to reduce a story down to its basic ideas or themes, that the action of *John Brown, Rose and the Midnight Cat* hinges on jealousy; *The Very Best of Friends* on one of the effects of grief; *A Bit of Company* (text also by Margaret Wild) on loneliness and *Willy the Wimp* on what happens when you try to change your self-image. This means that if you want to write about quite basic things – ideas that you might normally associate with literature for older children if not for adults, like death, fear, physical deterioration, envy or grief, for example – it is often perfectly possible to do so in the picture book form. Margaret Wild manages to write even about the liberation of a Nazi concentration camp in a form accessible to quite a young child in her recent title *Let the Celebrations Begin!* (also illustrated by Julie Vivas).

It is so irritating to be told when we are beginning that ideas are all around us. 'Where?' we cry in despair, longing to get started and with absolutely nothing in our heads. Yet really it is true. As Joan Aiken puts it in her

31

most helpful handbook, *The Way to Write for Children*, ideas are 'plentiful as blackberries in September' once we develop the ability to recognise them.

Try to keep a watch on yourself. Note which items on the news or in the newspaper are of particular interest to you, what serials you watch on television, perhaps, what articles you turn to in magazines when you are waiting at the dentist's, what leaps out at you from other people's conversation. Keep a notebook and jot down things that you notice, even if you haven't got the remotest idea of how they might be turned into stories. Cut out articles in the newspaper that seemed to you to be of interest. Remember that a story is really just looking at something from the inside, looking at an event which might be recorded in only a few words in a newspaper, imagining how it would have felt to have been the animal or the person concerned. How did the dog manage to cover all those miles to be reunited with its owner? How would the owner have reacted when he saw it? How would the wild dingo have felt coming starving, out of the flood areas, into the main street of a town?

You will start to become aware, perhaps to your surprise, of what you are most interested in. You may find that you are interested in schools, or in things to do with hospitals, or horses, or animals generally, or in how department stores are organised and run, or in train timetables. Perhaps you always had a secret desire to be a doctor or to run a horse stud, or whatever. Now is the time to take advantage of that interest, discover the details about it and use it as background for your stories.

The popular English novelist (for adults), Fay Weldon, claims that she has an idea for what could be a novel every morning when she wakes up. And once you start writing you too will find that you have more ideas than you know what to do with.

A great obstacle in the way of the beginning writer is the belief that you have to be original – in the sense of having a new idea. This didn't worry Shakespeare: he was perfectly happy to borrow his plot ideas from other sources. In an interesting chapter on ideas in her useful book *Writing Juvenile Stories and Novels*, Phyllis Whitney advises you, if you are stuck for one, to 'steal' someone else's. Work out what the underlying theme of a story is and then write your *own* version of it. There are plenty of stories about lost dogs or lost teddies, but that doesn't mean that there isn't room for one more: yours. Again there are many stories about a child moving into a new environment, perhaps to disrupt the pattern of relation-ships already established in a class or home, but how *you* write such a story, because of your personality, knowledge and language skills, will be quite different from anybody else's. It is a fresh and interesting *approach* that makes a story appear original, I suspect, and not its subject matter at all. Incidentally there are very few picture books set in the classroom that I can think of – Christobel Mattingley's *Black Dog* and the semi-factual *The Magic Schoolbus at the Waterworks* by Joanna Cole are the only ones that come readily to mind – so that is an area you might consider exploring for stories.

Some ideas do, however, seem to be particularly well suited to the picture book form. A story about a fear is one, for you have the problem and its resolution already there to provide you with an in-built structure. The story begins by stating the fear, and it will end with its abatement. It is really helpful to be able to see an easy structure like this for a picture book idea, for many ideas seem promising but just won't round themselves off neatly in the space.

There's a Sea in my Bedroom by Margaret Wild, illustrated by Jane Tanner, is an example of a picture book about a fear and how it is resolved. The child's problem and the seed of its resolution are given to the reader in the opening pages:

David was frightened of the sea.
It was a huge, wet monster that gobbled him up,
knocked him over, turned him upside down.

He didn't like the sea. Not at all, not one bit.

But he liked collecting shells.

One day he finds a conch shell with the sound of the sea inside. But this sea sounds 'soft and growly and friendly'. He takes the shell, with his pet sea inside it, and puts it in his bedroom. Then he starts to feel sorry for the sea, trapped in the shell. And he lets it out.

It's a simple but a very effective idea, and just right for a picture book. You might care to look at Margaret Barbalet's *The Wolf* (also illustrated by Jane Tanner) as an example of a much more complex (adult) treatment of the same theme. *There's an Alligator Under My Bed* by Mercer Mayer is another example of a picture book about a fear, although in this case the fear is shown to be resolved from the opening sentence: 'There used to be an alligator under my bed.' This prepares us for a humorous treatment of the idea.

Another kind of idea that seems to work well is one which deals with a palpable absurdity. The reader is put in the position of wanting to cry out to the characters that they aren't seeing what is obvious. A very simple example of this is *The Rain Puddle*, written by Adelaide

Holl and illustrated by Roger Duvoisin. It begins in this way:

Plump hen was picking and pecking
in the meadow grass.
*   "Cluck, cluck! Cluck, cluck!" she*
said softly to herself.

*   All at once, she came to a rain*
puddle.
*   "Dear me!" she cried. "A plump*
little hen has fallen into the water!"
*   And away she ran calling, "Awk,*
awk! Cut-a-cut! Cut-a-cut! Cut-a-
cut!"

*   Turkey was eating corn in the*
farmyard.
*   "Come at once!" called plump*
hen. "A hen is in the rain puddle!"
*   Away went turkey to see for*
himself.

The reader, even if only a young child, will soon become aware of what is going to happen next. He or she will become quite exasperated by the end of it as more and more animals come to look in the puddle and no one can guess the right answer. Children enjoy the feeling of power, of knowing more than the characters know. You might like to consider how Adelaide Holl could have resolved her story, and how you would have resolved it yourself.

A much more sophisticated version of the same kind of idea is the German book *The Bear Who Wanted to Stay a Bear,* written by Jörg Steiner and illustrated by Jörg Müller. This book, like *The Wolf*, also illustrates for us the wide range of difficulty in books for children, even within the picture book form. In this story the bear completes his winter hibernation only to find that his forest has disappeared and a factory is in its place. Even worse, he isn't recognised for what he is, and is forced to work in the factory, in blue overalls, just like any other employee. No one will take his story seriously: bears live in zoos or work in circuses, he is told. Even the bears in these places refuse to accept him:

*The circus bears looked at
the strange bear for a long,
long time.
    'He looks like a bear, but he
isn't a bear,' they said at
last. 'Bears don't sit in the
audience. Bears dance! Can
you dance?'
    'No,' said the bear, sadly.*

Again the reader is put in the position of wanting to give the answer: to say (indeed to scream out) by the end of it all, 'Look, of course he's a bear!' For the book, although humorous, is also very painful as well. The story is an allegory, and one that can speak, quite clearly, to a child who has just started school. It is about what we all have to do at times – prove our identity in an alien situation.

Obviously not all picture books deal with what is profound and indeed it would be a pity if they did. We don't want all our children's picture books to come loaded with messages and deeper meanings. Joan Aiken in *The Way to Write for Children*, suggests that we write about ordinary things within a small child's experience – like toast or stairs or blankets or even soap. Rod Clement in his book *Counting on Frank* does just this: he writes about ordinary things in a fresh and interesting way. 'I think about facts', says the boy in the story and then proceeds to inform us of ones we have certainly never thought of. In Jill Murphy's charming *Five Minutes' Peace* a mother (an elephant in curlers) longs to have just that short, blissful break – with the teapot and the newspaper – away from her loving but clamorous offspring.

Do have a look too at Shirley Hughes's picture books for examples of ordinary, everyday situations in pre-schoolers' lives turned into picture book material. In one story, for example, the pre-schooler gets locked inside the house while a growing number of neighbours and passing tradesmen try to help. My favourite out of all her warm stories about families is *Dogger*, based on the very common theme we never seem to grow tired of: the search for something lost. This time it is Dave's soft brown toy called Dogger. The opening pages of the story are really telling us that something will happen to him: he is described in detail, Dave's affection for him is made clear, and we are told about all the games Dave plays with him. We are also told that Dogger is the only toy that Dave likes. This kind of build-up is necessary in a story if we are to care about what will happen; we have to care about Dave, we have to like Dogger.

This is something which is hard to do when we are learning to write: we often like our characters, and don't want them to be uncomfortable. But this is what stories are all about. We have to make our characters unhappy so that they can achieve some sort of happiness or equilibrium at the end. Stories can, of course, move the other way, from happiness to unhappiness. But it is rare to shape a story in this way in books for the very young (although *I'll Always Love You* by Hans Wilhelm is one such example).

You will notice too, in *Dogger*, that Shirley Hughes doesn't make it too easy for Dave to get Dogger back. He finds him on the Toy Stall at the School Summer Fair with a ticket saying '5p', but of course Dave only has 3p in his pocket and has to go and find Mum and Dad, and while he is gone of course . . . I keep saying 'of course', because once you start writing stories you become aware of the barriers that other writers erect between a character and what he or she most desires. These are the techniques which annoy us as readers, in a way, but they do make us read on. In a story you can't make it too easy for your character to get what he wants: that's what I mean when I say you have to get used to making your character uncomfortable. Next time you watch a film or a serial on television, try to take note of the barriers, the hurdles, that the script-writers keep erecting all the time, and especially, in serials, at the end of each episode. Never think that you can only pick up techniques from children's writers or children's programmes. The techniques are the same, whatever the intended audience.

Don't feel either that what you write has to be true, that you must write about what actually happened. When you start really studying stories, so that you can write your own, you will find that quite a lot about them is elaborately contrived. Actual events are unlikely to provide you with a story structure. Nevertheless, a story that has its seed, its source, in something that really happened, is likely to ring true. Usually a blend of truth and fiction seems to work best.

A CONCENTRATED STYLE

Description

As I said earlier, a picture book text is not just a short, short story. It is a story written in a very condensed way with all the detail taken out of it but somehow lying just beneath the surface for the illustrator to find and develop. Consider the opening of *John Brown, Rose and the Midnight Cat*:

Rose's husband died a long time ago.
Now she lived with her dog.
His name was John Brown.

John Brown loved Rose,
and he looked after her in every way he could.

In summer he sat under the pear tree with her.
In winter he watched as she dozed by the fire.
All year round he kept her company.

Well, there isn't anything very special about that, you might think. But actually it needs a lot of discipline to write a text like this. What did the husband die of? How long ago was this? Were they happy together? What was he like? What sort of a dog is John Brown? How does he look after her? Oh the urge to put in all the detail about these points, to mention all the seasons at least. But Jenny Wagner has managed not to, and the result? A neat-looking picture book with few words and a happy illustrator who can supply all the material to answer these questions himself.

Or let's take a look at the opening of *The Friends of Emily Culpepper*:

In a quiet green valley is a village.

In the village is a row of cottages.

In the last cottage in the row lives Emily Culpepper.

You will notice how spare the text is, and how it advances half a step at a time. The last part of one sentence becomes the first part of the next, making early concentration on the story, before it gathers its own momentum, easy for the beginning reader. From a literary point of view, of course, it is a device that provides a simple and short build-up to what will be the main focus of the story, to Emily Culpepper herself. As you will find, the contented illustrator, Roland Harvey, supplies plenty of detail through the illustrations.

It is interesting, with this book, to work out just how much information is given to us by the illustrator, and how much by the writer. All the *text* has to tell us about Emily Culpepper is that she is 'an old lady who enjoys cooking and travelling . . .' Roland Harvey supplies the broomsticks.

If you are not very careful you will find that you are slipping into the style of the story book in your picture book text. As soon as you start putting in detail, become suspicious of yourself and see if there isn't a way to cut it down. I had a lot of trouble with the first paragraph of a picture book text that I wrote once called *Tatty*. I knew what I wanted to say, but the version I was working on sounded flat, lacking in rhythm, and I felt like giving up on an idea which initially I had thought was promising. This was that version:

Once there was a kitten called Charlotte.
She lived in a street where all the houses had lacy verandahs and
all the gardens had high walls.
Cats sat on these high walls.
Big cats called Pumpkin and Polar sat on the walls that should
have been Charlotte's.
"A wall is no place for a kitten," they said.
Charlotte looked up at them both and wished.
She was not a kind kitten so she wished that one day they would
fall off her walls.
This is the story of the day that happened.

That was what I wanted to say, in facts, but somehow
the style, the words, were wrong. The next time I had a
try at writing the story, I put away all the earlier drafts,
not looking at them, and tried to write the whole story
again from scratch. This is how the first paragraph
turned out:

Charlotte lived in a quiet street with Polar on one
side of her and Pumpkin on the other. All day they
sat on top of the walls that should have been Charlotte's
and told her what to do. At least Pumpkin told her what
to do and Polar told her what not to do. Sometimes she
got tired of it and wished that they would fall off the
walls that should have been hers.

This is shorter, and I hope, better, because this
became the final version for the book. It leaves out
unnecessary information. The illustrator could show us
that Charlotte is a kitten and Pumpkin and Polar large
cats. She also showed that this was an old suburb we
were talking about, so that there was no need to
mention the lacy verandahs and the high walls. By the

way, I found the walls a very useful framing device for the story, because it gave me a place where I could end, as well as begin.

Of course, if all this doesn't appeal to you, if you want to hang on to all your detail, then really it's a story book for children that you are interested in writing, and not a picture book text at all.

Dialogue

You are dealing with such a limited number of words in a picture book that you have to make the most of every one. Dialogue can be a way of doing two things simultaneously, if you put a bit of thought into it. Remember, as in all writing, dialogue should be a highlight.

Mem Fox, author of *Possum Magic*, is particularly good at showing the strength of a relationship in just a few words. Grandma Poss can't find the magic to make Hush visible again and the line that children sigh over, and rightly so, is this one:

"Don't worry Grandma," said Hush. "I don't mind."

This succinctly shows the relationship between them – we know that Hush really does mind very much indeed.

In *John Brown, Rose and the Midnight Cat* John Brown finds he has no breakfast and so he goes off in search of Rose:

'I'm sick,' said Rose. 'I'm staying in bed.'
'All day?' said John Brown.
'All day and for ever,' said Rose.

The little touch of 'for ever' immediately lifts the

story. It is humorous, in its exaggeration, but at the same time underlines the depths of Rose's depression.

Try to indicate personality through dialogue so that you convey information and portray your character at the same time. Perhaps the character has a tendency to repeat certain words and phrases, for example. In *Tatty*, both Pumpkin and Polar are bossy, but I tried to make Polar sound worse by making him always speak in negatives: ' "Common tabby is what we don't want here," said Polar.' Thursday, on the other hand, is a kindly, supportive cat, but a bit monumental, a bit slow and ponderous, so that when she speaks it's in half steps: she takes up what she has said in one sentence and extends it in the next:

"Make her a patch coat, then," said Thursday. "Patches will be better than nothing at all. Much better, with winter coming on."

Incidentally, notice the way in which you can get emphasis in a sentence just by the way you position the words: 'We don't want common tabby here,' is not nearly so strong as 'Common tabby is what we don't want here.'

REPETITION

Children really do love repetition in their stories, again, I think, because it gives them a feeling of power, of control, over the story. They know enough about what is going to happen next to make them feel comfortable. You can already see this element at work even in the short extract I quoted from *The Rain Puddle*. First the hen, then the turkey, and later a pig and a curly sheep come to stare into the rain puddle with predictable results. Jill Murphy makes use of this kind of structural repetition in several of her stories, including *Five Minutes' Peace*, *Peace at Last* and *On the Way Home*.

Children also love the sort of repetition that presents itself in the form of a chorus. Think of some famous repetitions. There is the 'But he was still hungry', of *The Very Hungry Caterpillar*. There is the refrain of Ping's list of many relatives in *The Story About Ping*:

Ping lived with his mother
and his father and two sisters and three brothers
and eleven aunts and seven uncles and forty-two
cousins.

And there is the irresistible refrain of the picture book published in 1929 and still selling fast, *Millions of Cats*:

Hundreds of cats,
Thousands of cats,
Millions and billions and trillions of cats.

It is a device which Rudyard Kipling uses again and again in his *Just So Stories*, often presented today in picture book form. 'The banks of the great grey-green greasy Limpopo River, all set about with fever-trees' is one of the well-loved refrains of 'The Elephant's Child'.

Some stories are, of course, more suited to refrains than others, but do keep this popular device in mind when you are constructing your story.

READING YOUR WORK ALOUD

I believe that all writing, of whatever kind, should read aloud well, and of course this is particularly important in literature for young children. When you first start to write you will perhaps be aware of how flat, how unconvincing, how distanced the writing sounds. You feel as though you want to get the words and make them stand up on the page. The way to do this is to keep telling your story, over and over again, until it sounds like someone talking to you, telling you the story, not like something written down at all. You may find that it helps to speak your story into a cassette recorder; this sometimes helps quite a bit. In most cases the nearer you can get to the sound of the spoken voice the better.

Beatrix Potter is an excellent model in this regard. Notice the very direct way in which she begins her famous story *The Tale of Jemima Puddle-Duck*:

What a funny sight it is
to see a brood of duck-
lings with a hen!
– Listen to the story of
Jemima Puddle-duck, who was
annoyed because the farmer's
wife would not let her hatch
her own eggs.

You not only get the sense of someone speaking to you, but almost of buttonholing you to come and listen to the story.

Any part of *The Tale of Peter Rabbit* has the same quality of directness:

Peter gave himself up for
lost, and shed big tears;
but his sobs were overheard by
some friendly sparrows, who
flew to him in great excite-
ment, and implored him to
exert himself.

Notice the use of language here as well: 'implored' and 'exert' are not common everyday words but are likely to be enjoyed by children because of that.

Russell Hoban is another, this time contemporary writer, whose picture book texts give you the sense of the spoken voice and whose words also have the lilt of poetry:

Once upon a time, before the Brute family
changed their name to Nice,
Sister Brute had nothing to love.

She had a mama and a papa.

She had a big brother and a baby brother.

"But I have nothing to love,"
said Sister Brute to her papa.
"May I have a doll?"

These lines are taken from the opening pages of *The Stone Doll of Sister Brute.*

TITLES

You can't really hope to attract the attention of a busy
editor unless you have an arresting title for your story.
Do take a lot of time and care over selecting a title that
not only suits your story but is likely to make an
impression. With a picture book, the publisher relies on
the cover and on the title to tempt a reader inside. Try
to think of titles which you have admired in books, or
which have become best-sellers like *Millions of Cats*, *The
Very Hungry Caterpillar*, *Leo the Late Bloomer* and *The Tale
of Jemima Puddle-Duck*.

STORY-TELLING

In a picture book, although it is so short, you still
require a story and a structure. You need to have a
beginning, a section where your conflict is developed,
and an ending. Since you are dealing with so few words
you really need to get into your story very quickly.
There is no room for sub-themes or for side-tracking of
any kind.

In her award-winning picture book, *The Very Best of
Friends*, Margaret Wild gets off to a quick start:

*Jessie and James lived on a farm with fifty
cattle, twenty chickens, four horses and three
dogs. But there was only one cat. William.*

At once you know that the animal which is important
in the story is the cat, since there is only one, since it is
named, because of its positioning in the paragraph, and

even by the full stop before 'William' which adds to its importance.

Again Beatrix Potter functions as a model for the effective and speedy beginning. On the first page of *The Tale of Peter Rabbit* we are introduced to all the major characters except one, and to where they live:

Once upon a time there
were four little Rabbits,
and their names were –
Flopsy,
Mopsy,
Cotton-tail,
and Peter.
They lived with their Mother
in a sand-bank, underneath the
root of a very big fir-tree.

On the second page we are given an outline of what is to be the plot, involving, as it does, the remaining main character:

'Now, my dears,' said old
Mrs. Rabbit one morn-
ing, 'you may go into the fields
or down the lane, but don't go
into Mr. McGregor's garden:
your Father had an accident
there; he was put in a pie by
Mrs. McGregor.'

Children will respond to this kind of story-telling: they are used to being told not to do things. The prohibition is also a very powerful story-telling device

for everybody: the room in *Bluebeard*, the 'don't look
back' in *Orpheus and Eurydice*, the 'don't eat' in the legend
of Persephone. In this, as in all the cases mentioned, it is
a prohibition associated with very real danger, and
children are likely to feel that this will be a genuinely
exciting story, dealing as it does with the possibility of
death.

I have already mentioned, in the discussion of *Dogger*,
the erecting of barriers, of hurdles, between your
character and what he or she desires the most. You will
notice Margaret Wild doing this in *The Very Best of Friends*
when Jessie finds herself ready to change towards William
but he, meanwhile, has changed away from her. You
must never have too easy a solution. Similarly in Josephine
Croser's *Tiddycat*, the child is given another cat when his
own cat dies. But, true to what often happens in life, it
is too soon for the child, and he hates the new cat.

Stories which succeed in ending with a twist can be
particularly effective. Ann Coleridge manages this in
The Friends of Emily Culpepper, where the policeman, in
his turn, ends up in a jar. Anthony Browne is similarly
successful in his much-loved picture book *Willy the
Wimp*, where we find that it is not so easy to change our
personalities after all. And see if you can guess who
screams at the end of Margaret Wild's *A Bit of Company*.

Felix and Alexander by Terry Denton works well as a
story because it is based on a reversal of roles: the
stuffed toy Felix saves his master Alexander who has
become lost in the darkness of the city. Perhaps you
could think of a variant of this. Try taking a usual idea
and giving it a twist like this.

Remember too, that above all else, a story must *convince*.
Often it is the little touches which help to do this. Beatrix
Potter first simply describes how Peter gets caught in a

gooseberry net because of the size of the buttons on his jacket. And then she elaborates on the jacket: 'It was a blue jacket with brass buttons, quite new.' Such a sentence somehow convinces you of the truth of the whole story because the writer is prepared to hold up the narrative in order to fill you in on the details.

This might appear to be contradicting what I said earlier about not putting in detail that can be shown in the illustrations. But the description here actually has a dual function: it is important to the plot as well. The sentence is being used to alert the child reader to possible trouble over the jacket later. (Where the writer is also the illustrator, as here, we may take it that any detail like this is probably performing a special function within the story as a whole.) In a sense too Beatrix Potter's books stand between the modern spare form of the picture book text and what we now call the story book: *The Tale of Peter Rabbit* is 963 words long and *The Tale of Jemima Puddle-Duck* 1300 words.

Strong emotion will also help 'carry' a story and convince us of its 'truth': in Anthony Browne's cleverly understated *Gorilla*, for example, where a child longs for her father's company, or in Hans Wilhelm's *I'll Always Love You* where the child learns gradually that his dog's lifetime is to be so much shorter than his own.

VISUALISING

Some stories will, of course, illustrate much more easily than others. You will notice this on the television news, or on factual programmes, where at times the camera is at a loss to find a picture for a segment. It is wise to try to visualise your story as you proceed from paragraph to paragraph – just to check that it can, in fact, be illustrated. I would keep this aspect in mind but not *too* strongly, for some stories which don't seem to be particularly visual *do* work well in the hands of a clever illustrator, like *John Brown, Rose and the Midnight Cat*.

Consider this part of *The Very Best of Friends*:

Then one Sunday morning James died,
suddenly, of a heart attack.

That doesn't seem a very promising segment for an illustrator yet Julie Vivas has made of this, one of her very best pictures. She conveys the sadness that accompanies James's death simply by drawing the defenceless, pathetic-looking backs of Jessie and all the creatures as they watch the ambulance drive away.

It is as well to remember that even if you do carefully visualise each segment, this is not the way in which your illustrator may see the story. Usually authors have very little say in the illustration of their work although this does vary from publisher to publisher. Where a factual mistake has been made in the illustration (for example, where a house has been depicted as green when it was described in the text as red) it is often the writer who is asked, on the grounds of speed, to alter the text to match the illustration and not the other way round. It is not the writer's responsibility to find an illustrator; this is a common misapprehension. It is the publisher who will find an artist whose work will match the kind of story that it is and the style of the writing.

DRAFTS

It is a mistake to think that clear, lucid writing which appears effortless is in fact so. Clear, concentrated writing is usually the result of much effort. The effort is in making it appear effortless. Most stories are the result of many drafts. Interestingly too, it seems that the longer the story, the fewer drafts that are needed. A writer may be content with three drafts of a novel, six to nine of a story book for younger readers, and twelve to twenty odd for a picture book. This makes sense, really, in that there are so few words in the picture book that they have to be exactly right. Where you hear of a book being produced in a very short time, like Michael Bond's *A Bear Called Paddington* in a week, or D. H. Lawrence's *Sea and Sardinia* in six weeks, it is because there is a long history of writing behind them. The author has been writing regularly for years so that fluency with words is there just waiting to be tapped when an irresistible idea comes along.

If you are working on an idea which you still believe in, but it doesn't seem to be writing up well, put all your previous drafts away and start again from scratch. This will often work quite well, because all the basic material that you want in your story is in your head. It always helps to see what material keeps coming up in draft after draft when you are not looking at the previous draft as you type in the new one. This shows you which parts of your story are really essential to you. Don't throw away your earlier attempts either. You will want to go through them later and tick the parts which are better expressed than in your later versions. It is always a good idea to date each draft so that you can follow the progress of your story.

RHYMED PICTURE BOOKS

These do seem to be very popular with children. Only use this form, however, if it seems the best way of putting across your idea. And don't use it at all if you haven't developed an ear yet for poetic rhythms.

The main rule for doing it well is not to let the rhyme or rhythm govern what you have to say. Work out what you want to say first in prose, divide your material up into logical steps, and then write a verse for each step. Choose a simple rhyme scheme and stick to it. Make sure you are keeping to the same rhythm. And please do say each verse aloud, checking that it is in fact flowing, not halting along lamely like quite a few published picture book texts. One clear way of avoiding this is not to let any stress within a line fall on an unimportant word like 'in', for example, which we would not normally emphasise in speech. It is even worse to let the stress fall on the wrong syllable of a word, so that the reader is forced to say it unnaturally – some*thing* instead of *some*thing. You must not put a word where it attracts the opposite stress.

For models here I wouldn't use rhymed picture books because they vary so much in quality. Rather, I would suggest that you study the poetry of Walter de la Mare. He is notably one of the poets who reminds us of the possibilities of language, particularly its rhythm. Be haunted by lines like these:

'The Truants'

Ere my heart beats too coldly and faintly
To remember sad things, yet be gay,
I would sing a brief song of the world's little children
Magic hath stolen away.

The primroses scattered by April,
The stars of the wide Milky Way,
Cannot outnumber the hosts of the children
Magic hath stolen away.

And if you want models for the skilled use of rhyme and rhythm with humour, who better than Roald Dahl or our own Max Fatchen?

The Wolf stood there, his eyes ablaze
And yellowish, like mayonnaise.
His teeth were sharp, his gums were raw,
And spit was dripping from his jaw.

Or

Please say a word for rhubarb,
It hasn't many chums
For people like banana splits
Or fancy juicy plums.

They slice the sweet, sweet melon
Or gather tasty pears,
But if you mention rhubarb pie
You get the rhudest stares.

The second extract is from 'Be Nice to Rhubarb' by Max Fatchen in his *Songs for My Dog and Other People*; the first is from 'The Three Little Pigs' in Roald Dahl's extraordinary collection *Revolting Rhymes*.

Roald Dahl, sad to say, is now dead. On hearing the news one of the children at our local primary school said: 'He *can't* die!' I should think words like these would be echoing all round the world.

Remind yourself of what poetry can be like by reading the verses of Tennyson and Keats, for example, Yeats and Hopkins and Shakespeare. Read verses like these:

Full fathom five thy father lies;
  Of his bones are coral made;
Those are pearls that were his eyes:
  Nothing of him that doth fade,
But doth suffer a sea-change
  Into something rich and strange . . .

(From Shakespeare's *The Tempest*)

The trees are in their autumn beauty,
The woodland paths are dry,
Under the October twilight the water
Mirrors a still sky . . .

(From the opening of 'The Wild Swans at Coole' by W. B. Yeats)

Just remember that the poet, in common with all writers, has to value not only the meaning but the *sound* of words. Perhaps I could just conclude with Walter de la Mare's poem about his joy in this. Do read his 'Words' aloud!

'Words'

How I love the rhymes that I can dance to, sing to –
Sing to, dance to, and echoing with birds!
Rhymes that, like bells, the mind may chime and ring to,
Elf-bells, steeple-bells – sweet-tongued words.

TRY THIS!

- Write a picture book text of about 500 words on one of the following:

  a child's game
  a friendship
  a quest

  (You may find it helpful to organise your story into 14 or 15 simple paragraphs.)

- Write fifteen short rhymes suitable for a picture book text about

  a shop
  or
  an animal
  or
  a journey.

- Comment on the qualities of a picture book text which you admire. It may be one mentioned in this chapter, but not necessarily so.

- Start an 'ideas' scrap-book. (See p. 32)

CHAPTER 4

Story Books (6–10 Years)

This is a very exciting area for the beginning writer, or indeed for any writer at all. Here you have the opportunity to utilise all the aspects of story but in a clear and uncluttered way. When I think of books for younger readers I think of clean lines – like a simply structured ship or building. It should be possible to see the structure of such a story quite easily, in a way that is not possible in the denser, more complex books after this. These books are certainly simpler, but they must not be watered down. Again, how we fulfil our obligation to children is by writing in the best possible way we can.

In some ways this is an easier form to write in than the picture book. Certainly it is easier as far as language use goes. You can now use language more naturally, just as it flows. You don't need to observe the concentration of the picture book style where every word has to be in its right place and every word has to count.

In some ways, however, it is harder. It is now that you really have to come to grips with the problem of developing your material. The way to do this is to expand upon one small idea, not throw in more and more ideas in order to achieve length.

I think it is in some ways harder than the novel for older readers too. As the protagonist becomes older, so is it easier for writers to put in thoughts and feelings that are basically their own. When you are writing from the point of view of a young child, a careful screening process has to be in place. The younger the child, the more difficult point of view becomes.

This is an area which covers such a wide age range that you would expect to find many levels of difficulty within it. (Keep in mind too that it is perfectly possible to read many of these books to children younger than six.) As I mentioned before, you will find that print size is quite a useful guide to the actual age (or perhaps we should say the actual reading age) the publisher has in mind. The quantity of illustration is another indicator.

Let's remind ourselves now of the general characteristics of the form.

BASIC CONSIDERATIONS

Length

Books vary greatly in length and format. At the younger end of the scale these are often virtually picture books with extended texts (as we noted in Chapter 2). Two of the books on the Children's Book Council of Australia's 1991 shortlist for Younger Readers were in this form: *Boris and Borsch* (written by Robin Klein and illustrated by Cathy Wilcox) and *Mervyn's Revenge* (Leone Peguero and Shirley Peters). Often the same story could be presented either as a picture book with an extended text, or as a short story book. It really depends on the publisher.

The 'Dipper' series by Omnibus Books is an example of such short story books intended for beginning readers. These are small, copiously illustrated books whose texts range from about 1500 to 2500 words, like *The Follow Dog* by Sally Farrell Odgers (illustrated by Noela Young) or *Squawk and Screech* by Gillian Rubinstein and illustrated by Craig Smith.

There are other such series published in England like Hamish Hamilton's Gazelle books and the Julia MacRae series mentioned earlier. These are recognisable by their large print, large spaces between the lines and numerous illustrations as being intended for the beginning reader; but the length here tends to range from 3000 to 6000 words, at least in the latter series.

Young Puffins include titles for the beginning and for the more advanced young reader. Stories can be as short as 2500 words (the length of my *Pomily's Wish* – I can't think of another one as short!) or as long as 13,000 or 14,000 words (the lengths respectively of Morris Lurie's highly popular *The 27th Annual African Hippopotamus Race* and Christobel Mattingley's *Duck Boy*). Young Lions (HarperCollins) is a similar series. Angus & Robertson's Blue Gum imprint includes many titles for the 8 to 10s like *Danny's Egg* by Colin Thiele.

Beginning writers tend to worry a lot about length, and certainly if you are trying to write a story that will fit into a particular series, like the 'Dipper' one, it is important to keep length in mind. However, as you can see, it is really possible to market a story of almost any length from say, 1000 words up to 14,000 or even more, for younger readers. (*Finders Keepers*, the winner of the 1991 Younger Readers' Award, must be well past this length.) It is probably best, then, to write your story as competently and succinctly as you can and then worry about marketing it later.

Sentence structure

Obviously you have to be more concerned about sentence structure in books at the younger end of this age range. But even here, this doesn't mean that your sentences must all be short or uniformly structured. It does mean that where your sentences are longer you should try to use fairly central and clear connectives. Don't be afraid of 'and' and 'but', for example. These are the conjunctions most used in Beatrix Potter's tales and make a story easy to follow for the younger reader.

In a way this all seems more of a problem than it really is. You will find that your choice of subject matter and point of view will to a large extent dictate an appropriate style for your story. The same may be said for vocabulary.

Vocabulary

Here the writer is much better advised to be guided by the requirements of the story he or she is writing, rather than by thinking that the language has to be watered down in some way to suit the needs of the audience. The best rule is the same one as we applied in the picture book area: use the words that seem best for your story, that convey your ideas in the most vivid and interesting way. The following words are taken from a well-known book for young children: *convenient, elegantly, alighted, superfluous, retired, hospitable, suffocating, immensely, conscientious, tedious, savoury, simpleton, suspicious, snippets, awe, burdened, abrupt, escorted.* And the book? *The Tale of Jemima Puddle-Duck* by Beatrix Potter.

IDEAS

Use of contrast

Stories based on a simple contrast often work well. In Robin Klein's *The Enemies*, the mothers like each other but the children don't. In *Boris and Borsch* by the same author, the two boys Eugene and Patrick, are opposites as are their households, and so are the two bears, Boris and Borsch. You then just have to make sure that the boys get the wrong bears and you are off to an interesting start. 'Black Eyes', a short story by Philippa Pearce, is an earlier powerful and sinister treatment of the same idea.

A change in situation

You can also have contrast used in the development of a situation. In *No Pets Allowed* by Edel Wignell, Amy tries to take her cat Toff to the caravan park and is unhappy because she is caught. Liz is even more unhappy because she succeeds in taking her poodle Pierre but hasn't realised what the consequences are likely to be.

More fundamentally, your child may have to change schools, or towns, or countries, or go and live with an aunt or grandparent. Perhaps he or she has to adjust to a new brother or sister in the family or to a cousin or grandparent who has come to stay. From being rich, the family may become poor, or vice versa.

A simple adventure

Stories can be based on a simple adventure. In some ways this is easier to arrange in a story for young children if your characters are animals or toys. The toy or animal can be lost or ill-treated or simply left behind. It is of course possible to think up a satisfying (realistic) adventure story involving children. Joan Phipson succeeded with this in her *Hide Till Daytime*, where a brother and sister are locked inside a large department store at closing time. In Jane Gardam's *Bridget and William* Bridget and her pony William have to find their way alone through the snow-drifts and over the seven gates to the village and the doctor.

Often writers will introduce a fantasy element into stories for the age group in order to satisfy this need for adventure. In each of Emily Rodda's books for young children an object transports the child into a fantasy world: in *Something Special* it is old clothes gathered for a jumble sale; a piece of paper with a drawing on it in *Pigs Might Fly*; a carousel that mysteriously appears on a vacant block in *The Best-kept Secret*; a television set in *Finders Keepers*.

A position of superiority

A successful idea for this age group, as with the picture book text, is one where children feel in a position of superiority to the characters. This is one of the reasons for the appeal of *Winnie-the-Pooh*, of course, which is about the adventures of *a Bear of Very Little Brain*. *Rhyming Russell*, by Pat Thomson and Caroline Crossland, about the boy who cannot help but speak in rhyme, might be another such example.

An animal at the centre of some conflict

A boy might find a stray animal, but the family doesn't want to keep it. He may be offered a pet, but not the one he has in mind. He falls in love with the *idea* of having a pet, and not with the pet itself. A girl may love a horse, but it belongs to someone else. She sees an animal being abused and feels helpless. She wants to keep a pet yet at the same time not interfere with its freedom.

Reversals

Stories which are based on some kind of reversal are often very successful, like Anne Fine's *The Country Pancake*. Lance worries a lot about his teacher, Miss Mirabelle, who behaves like a naughty child. She is inappropriately dressed, often bored (even when the class find the work interesting!) and won't do her job. Much of her time is spent in gazing out of the window.

POINT OF VIEW

Point of view, as you may remember, refers to the position from which a story is told: through whose eyes we experience the action.

Omniscient

In stories for the very young it is often easiest to make use of the omniscient point of view, the viewpoint that you will be familiar with from the fairy-tale, for example. Here you, as the writer, know everything about your characters, are able to pop in and out of everybody's mind, comment on everybody's feelings, and generally move around in your story as you see fit. Such a viewpoint allows you to summarise easily, which is very important where words are at a premium – as they are when you are writing a story for beginning readers. One way to put it might be that you are writing the story from the outside, looking down on the action.

You need to make use of this point of view where

stories deal with protagonists who don't know enough and haven't got the words to tell the story convincingly themselves – stories with a very young child as protagonist, or with protagonists like birds. Gillian Rubinstein makes use of this viewpoint in her delightful book for beginning readers, *Squawk and Screech*. The story opens in a brisk, no-nonsense way, rapidly summarising material:

Squawk was a musk lorikeet, noisy, hand-some and quarrelsome – a hero in the world of birds. He lived for many years around Sleeps Hill, where his territory ran from the quarry to the school. He raised many noisy, handsome, quarrelsome chil-dren. But after several years of summer and winter, drought and rain, he became slower and less wary.

Later we will be permitted to see into the thoughts and feelings of Squawk and Screech (a second musk lorikeet), the bird woman and the burglar, but the whole story is held together by the dominant point of view that can see everything and go everywhere.

First-person narrator
You may wish to tell your story directly, through the eyes of a child (or an animal or a toy) who appears to be yourself. Many stories for children of all ages are in the first person, including those for younger readers. Max Dann's *Adventures with My Worst Best Friend* is one such example. Many of Paul Jennings's stories, including *The Paw Thing* and *The Cabbage Patch Fib*, are presented like this. The first-person narrator may be your main

character or may simply be a way of mediating someone else's story – as Chris's brother does, in the last-mentioned title. The form has the great advantage of immediacy, of someone speaking directly to you, and it is very often used in humorous writing for this age group.

It has several disadvantages, however, or rather difficulties connected with its use. If you use the first person it is very important that you *sound* like, that you appear to catch the idiom, of the eight-year-old boy or the nine-year-old girl. If you think about it, you will see that it is a form almost impossible to use with a child much younger than this as a protagonist. It is possible, though, to use it with animals – they are often adults in disguise in any case.

It is a form where you have to be very careful about *tone*. Some first-person stories for children seem very forced, facetious rather than funny, where you get the impression that the writer is producing something which he or she thinks 'will be okay for kids'. 'Tone' reflects our attitude to our audience: if we think that in some way we are superior to our child readers our opinion is sure to show through in our style.

Another problem is in giving your first-person narrator a personality. Some writers are very successful at this: Jessica in *A Long Way from Verona* by Jane Gardam and Erica in *Hating Alison Ashley* by Robin Klein are characters who come readily to mind. But these examples are taken from older age categories. It is harder to think of memorable first-person narrators in stories for younger readers – although a notable exception is Nam-Huong in Diana Kidd's cleverly structured *Onion Tears*. But often the narrator is simply used as a viewpoint onto the story – not colouring it by his or her perspective at all.

It is also difficult to praise your character in forms discreet enough not to put your reader off.

Third-person narrator

With this approach you also limit yourself to what one character can see, hear and understand, but in some ways it is harder to do than the first person. It is easy to slip out of your character's viewpoint and into the omniscient point of view without even noticing. It can be a very frustrating form because of the need to preserve this single viewpoint on events. It has many advantages, however.

First of all it simulates our own experience in life (as does the first-person viewpoint but without having its disadvantages). We too are often puzzled by events and wonder about the motives and actions of others. It is therefore a very satisfactory form for creating mysteries and generating misunderstandings.

It is the form in which it is easiest to create an emotional identification between your character and your reader. Intensity is created if we keep inside the one character's thoughts and perspective; it tends to be lost if we shift outside the character.

A combination of viewpoints

In books for very young children it is difficult to use the third-person narrator form exclusively because of the helplessness and lack of knowledge of the main protagonist. You may find it necessary to combine it with the omniscient point of view. It is common for writers to begin their stories with the omniscient viewpoint to set the scene, describe the characters and give the germ of the plot. In Chapter 2 they will often then slip gradually into the viewpoint of the main protagonist. This was what I did in *Heffalump?* where the arrival of the toy and the reason for him being given such a name is made clear in Chapter 1. In Chapter 2, I then moved into the mind of the toy, giving Heffalump?'s experiences from his own point of view.

CHARACTERISATION

Main characters
Stories for younger children will probably work best if you have just a few characters, the underlying principle being that you don't want to introduce more material than it is possible to develop adequately. Many writers will have just one or at most two or three main characters, with others introduced but kept more or less in the background.

It is always quite helpful to have a male and a female protagonist, if this fits in with your idea. If you have two main characters of the same sex it's easy to get into a tangle with lots of only 'hes' or 'shes', so that your reader becomes unsure of whom you are talking about. It's sensible also not to make the names of your characters too similar.

Writers, as we have seen, often make use of contrasting characters. This makes it easier for readers to keep the characters clearly in their minds. It is also likely to result in plenty of conflict – as it does in Jan Mark's beautifully developed short novel (8500 words) *The Dead Letter Box*.

Her main characters are Louie and Glenda, although, interestingly enough, Glenda appears directly in the story on only a few occasions. Louie is imaginative, a reader, not popular, and tends to cast herself in the role of one who is hardly done by, like her mother. Glenda, by contrast, has a literal mind. She reads (if she must) comics; she is popular, always knows what everything costs, and is quite unemotional. She in turn often sounds like *her* mother: bossy and impatient and with little regard for the feelings of others.

You will notice that the contrast is in personality and not in more superficial aspects like appearance. You will have to work out for yourself how important it is for your story to put in physical descriptions of your characters. It is perfectly possible to do without these altogether, as Jan Mark seems to here, with the illustrations filling in this kind of detail. I believe it is a mistake to put in too much physical description before your reader has had a chance to become interested in the characters as personalities. Early descriptions of freckles, hair colour, height and so on will have no impact.

'Lightning' character sketches

'Lightning' character sketches, however, are different. These are the ones that are put in to describe very quickly a background character or group of characters. Such descriptions give body to a story, like this one of Louie's class:

. . . *now Louie had to share with Wayne Hodges, who wore his snorkel jacket indoors and sat with the hood zipped up, so that he looked like a ship's ventilator. Glenda was over by the window with Sarah and Helen Tate who were twins and talked only to each other, and Joanne Smith who sucked her pigtails and never talked at all.*

Another that I particularly like is of the 'big hand-woven lady with four dribbly children' whom Louie sees in the library. The 'hand-woven' in association with 'big', seems to suggest that the woman is wearing something not entirely suited to her, and the 'four dribbly children' perhaps suggests a further messiness, even an inability to cope.

When you are doing your lightning sketches it is sensible to choose something arresting, something unusual or humorous rather than commonplace, for you are trying to indicate character very succinctly. Jane Austen is a master of the technique as here, in her opening description of Lady Bertram in *Mansfield Park*:

She was a woman who spent her days in sitting nicely dressed on a sofa, doing some long piece of needle-work, of little use and no beauty, thinking more of her pug than her children . . .

This sentence is quite sufficient to establish her character for the duration of the novel.

Use of a toy as a character

If you have a toy as a protagonist it will basically behave as a person in that it will think and feel. It may not have freedom of movement, however. It is always a good idea to establish rules about what your toy can and cannot do. It may be able to understand what people say, but not be able to speak to them. It may be able to move of itself, but only in the dark, or at midnight, or whatever. Perhaps its personality is determined by the kind of toy that it is or by the treatment that it has had. Restrictions like these actually *help* to develop a story – not impede it, as you might think. *The Mouse and His Child* by Russell Hoban is an excellent example of restrictions producing strength.

Use of an animal as a character

It is interesting to notice the variety of ways in which animals are presented in children's stories. They may simply be presented as animals, as we know them in life. More often, they are characterised virtually as people. The author knows what they think and feel; they talk, perhaps only amongst themselves, and they have human fears and aspirations. In E. B. White's *Charlotte's Web*, Wilbur is shown in the opening chapter simply as a pig. It is the little girl, Fern, whom we are invited to become interested in. As the story moves on, however, we leave Fern behind and become involved in the activities of the animals on the farm. Wilbur now becomes the child of the story while Charlotte the spider, and Templeton the rat, become the adults.

PLOT: HOW TO DEVELOP YOUR IDEAS

Using point of view

First decide on your point of view.

You might remember our idea of a boy having to go and live with a grandparent. Why does he have to go? What has happened in his family? When you can answer these questions you have your initial situation which you may reveal at the beginning of your story; alternatively, you may decide to hold it back. Suppose that when he gets there, he finds that there is another child the grandparent seems to be closer to. Maybe it is the girl next door who has been taking his grandfather's dog for a walk and generally keeping him company. There is plenty of scope here for rivalry and conflict, and conflict is what stories (and plots) are all about.

Now you could tell this story from the point of view of the child who comes to stay with the grandparent. You may wish, however, to tell it from the viewpoint of the child next door. This latter approach might in fact help you to create mysteries about the child who has come – about *why* he has come, for the grandfather is unlikely to confide in her.

Then you have to think of incidents that will bring the two children together. Probably the grandfather thinks that they will be delighted to have each other's company, and so he deliberately engineers this. It seems likely that they will dislike each other at first – maybe they always will, that's up to you. You may want to have two boys or two girls; you may prefer to have a grandmother or an aunt. The grandparent may live in the country and the child in the city, or vice versa. Three main characters should be all that you are likely to need.

The incidents will probably arise from the personalities and interests of the children. Maybe the next-door child resents having her hobbies and interests intruded upon. Perhaps during one of their fights they manage to lose the dog between them, and blame each other or else they forget about their differences and co-operate at last.

Dividing your material up into chapters

It probably helps at this stage to organise your ideas into chapters if it seems likely that your story will be long enough for this. It already looks as though the one we are playing with will be. These chapters can be really short – perhaps just a page or two of type. Presenting a story in chapters helps the reader and the writer. It assists readers by providing them with (small) milestones throughout the story. It also assists writers with their story-telling: each chapter has to end at a point where the reader will want to move on. Chapter endings are, in fact, an excellent way of maintaining tension and indeed of generating suspense. A study of Emily Rodda's chapter endings will help you with this: she is very skilled at making you want to read on. Consider the effect of this one from *The Best-kept Secret*, where Joanna looks down from the magic carousel:

Joanna lifted her head and looked quickly and fearfully over the side. She saw a blurred picture of Marley Street. Marley Street, with its shops, its people, its trees, dead still. Nothing moved. Not a leaf, or a shadow. It was like a video when someone has pushed the "pause" button, or like a film, frozen at a single moment. Everything was wispy round the edges, faint and blurred. And there was no sound at all. Like a lift stuck between floors the carousel sat dumb, useless and inert, while its passengers looked at one another in growing panic, knowing they were trapped, and helpless.

Handling of plot

Let's look now at how Jan Mark handles plot in *The Dead Letter Box*.

The plot of this novel arises from the sharply contrasting characters of Louie and Glenda (referred to above) and deals with a not unfamiliar situation in children's lives: what happens when your best friend leaves your town and your school? The twist that Jan Mark gives to this plot idea is that it is not altogether clear that Glenda *is* Louie's best friend, or indeed any kind of friend at all. Glenda and Louie (we are told at the beginning of the story),

were best friends, but Glenda was Louie's only friend, while everybody was Glenda's friend. Glenda might start talking to almost anyone, even if Louie were already talking to her.

We begin to realise that this, and similar passages, are slanted in that they are given to us through Louie's perceptions of the situation. In Louie's eyes Glenda is a genuine friend, but at best it is only indifference that Glenda shows to her throughout. 'I can't stand around here all day,' she says to Louie, just before she is about to move permanently to another town, 'talking about old films.'

Although it is clear to the reader that Glenda is not at all upset about leaving Louie (indeed, at the thought of change, she is as excited as a person like Glenda can ever be), Louie persists for most of the novel in being deeply upset about Glenda's going away and in the attempt to find ways of keeping in touch with her. The plot centres on these ways and on Louie's gradual realisation that she has been wasting her emotion and her friendship on Glenda.

After watching a spy film, Louie hits on the idea of having a dead letter box – which is to be a book that is never borrowed in the public library – and she and Glenda are to leave messages for one another there. Except that, predictably, (but not for Louie) Glenda forgets all about it, and all that Louie finds on repeated visits is her own letter. So she writes Glenda a new letter:

Dear Glenda,

I think you are a
Mean Rotten Old Thingy and
I never did like you. Im
GLAD you moved. I wish
you moved years ago. They
have painted your house
HORRIBLE RED all
over and thrown the
bird bath away. I hope
you DONT EVER
come back.
     Love from Louie.

Apart from the humour here, the reader is aware of Louie's heartache and also of her realisation that Glenda's 'friendship' has actually always represented very little. Fortunately she has recently found a proper, reliable friend in the library, Jane Garland, and although she is only on holiday from London, that turns out to be an advantage too; now Louie has a proper pen-friend, one who will actually write letters to her.

In this little book there are six chapters:

Chapter 1   Initial situation. Glenda is leaving.

Chapter 2   The spy film and the idea for the dead letter box.

Chapter 3   Finding an unpopular book in the local library and making it the dead letter box.

Chapter 4   Glenda leaves and Louie plants the letter.

Chapter 5   Louie finds her own letter in the library.
             She meets Jane.

Chapter 6   The idea of writing notes in books catches
             on. Louie cements her friendship with Jane.

Christobel Mattingley is another writer (South Australian
this time) who can help us with the structuring of our
stories. She is a very clear, careful story-teller and we
can learn a lot from her novel *Duck Boy* about how to
develop a simple idea into book length for younger
children.

When Adam goes for a holiday on a farm with his
older brother and sister, Steve and Kate, he finds that he
gets left out of everything worth doing. Steve takes over
the one-man canoe and spends his time on the river while
Kate takes over the only horse. It looks as if Adam's
holiday will be miserable, spent in looking after the
chooks and helping Mrs Perry in the kitchen – until he
gets interested in the ducks, Lucy and General. He thinks
Lucy must be sick because she sits all the time down at
the creek, but Mrs Perry tells him that Lucy 'must be
broody. Poor dears, they try so hard, but they never
succeed in raising a family. Something always happens.'

It then becomes Adam's task to prevent the
'something' from happening this time. Steve and Kate,
of course, are ready to ridicule him, 'wasting' his
holiday worrying about ducks.

In the course of the story, Adam watches the nest
while he learns to swim in the creek, saves Lucy's
thirteen eggs from a goanna, and guards against rats and
foxes by building an enclosure for the ducks out of
netting and droppers. He even digs a trench and buries
the base of the wire. His hard work, which includes a

night visit to check on Lucy during a storm, is rewarded threefold, for the duck brings out nine of her eggs, Steve is impressed with what he has done and allows him to take the canoe, and Kate lets him ride on Daisy.

If you study the way in which, with careful detail, Christobel Mattingley has developed her initial idea, you may soon get some sense of how to do it yourself. The book is divided into nine chapters, each chapter, apart from the first and the last, developing some aspect of Adam's task in trying to protect Lucy and her eggs.

LANGUAGE

Description

Now that you are writing at greater length (compared with the picture book) it is perfectly possible to include passages of description in your story, and although these are for younger readers, there is no need to water down your prose style because of this. A concentrated effect can be achieved if you try to relate your descriptions to other aspects of the story.

Consider this passage from Jean Kenward's *Ragdolly Anna*, a model of clear, simple, yet vivid writing which in addition relates to the main subject matter of the book:

And there was the river itself. Ragdolly
Anna had not imagined it would be so big or so
beautiful. She had not guessed it would be
moving gently all the time, as if it were going
somewhere and was not to be put off on any
account. All over the surface were crinkly marks

and patterns. There were lilies, too, yellow ones
with long writhing stalks like snakes, and round
leaves like dinner plates. And underneath the
water, if you looked down, you could see swarms
of tiny fish as thin as pins, darting about together;
and sometimes, a large, speckled one, thoughtful
and lazy, lying still next to a stone – only the
occasional movement of a fin told you that it was
a fish at all.

The peace of the scene enters into every line. Notice
how the writer moves from the more general aspects of
the scene – the movement of the river and its size – to
the more particular aspects: the surface patterns, the
lilies, and then to the perspective under the water, from
'swarms of tiny fish' to the single, speckled, thoughtful
one. And not only peace, but wonder, for the tone of the
passage derives from Ragdolly Anna who has seen
nothing like this before. The comparisons the writer
makes are well within the experience of a young child,
yet accurate at the same time, the 'round leaves like
dinner plates' and 'swarms of tiny fish as thin as pins',
for example. The latter description is particularly apt
since Ragdolly Anna is a dressmaker's doll.

What follows is a favourite passage of mine from Jane
Gardam's *Bridget and William*:

Far to either side of it [the track] there was a
dot here and a dot there – low farms
with smoke rising. Purple heather
came rolling in to the dale bottoms
to the sharp edges of bright green
fields – squares and oblongs and
strips and one field the shape of a

boot. Then the track disappeared
over a brow near the Saxon Cross
and even beyond that you could not
see the village. Just a bluebell haze
and white clouds hurtling. There
were seven white gates along this
lovely road. Bridget imagined a
horse trotting.

One of the main reasons for exposing young children to Jane Gardam's books is because of her skill with words. Her style has the clarity and freshness which can only be arrived at after much thought and labour, and is just as remarkable in her books for her youngest as for her older readers. It is also a very concentrated prose. Notice how she omits words in her descriptions: 'low farms with smoke rising' and 'Just a bluebell haze and white clouds hurtling', for example. Words like rolling in, rising, hurtling and trotting give an effect of animation to the scene and 'one field the shape of a boot' creates a homely effect.

This passage does not simply relate to setting, however, and this is what I mean about concentration of effect. The seven white gates, although introduced here so simply and disarmingly, are to prove crucial to the plot and structuring of the story.

A binding image

Even in a book for very young children it is possible to use a technique often used in books for older readers including, of course, adults: this is the use of an image to help hold the story together and keep it vividly in the reader's mind. Bernard Ashley makes use of this technique in *Linda's Lie*.

Linda has a yellow canary and throughout the story the canary image is used to explain what is happening to her in Linda's terms. Early in the story she speaks of her father throwing a 'cover over the whole idea' (of her going to the ballet) 'like putting the yellow canary to sleep for the night'. Linda is ashamed of not having the money to go to the ballet like the other children and she lies about it, one lie leading inevitably to the next. One night she cries under her blanket and suddenly realises how her silent canary must feel – 'covered and trapped: only she was in a cage of lies'.

The story ends with a happy image, still of the canary, as Linda returns to the classroom where the music of the ballet is playing:

She glided into it with a lightness
and a joy that only she could know
about – like a happy bird with the
cover off, suddenly released to dance
free in the sky.

This simple use of a motif gives a pictorial representation to Linda's moral plight and helps bind the story together, keeping its main theme clear in a child's mind.

Dialogue

In the story book it is necessary to open up your scenes through action and dialogue. Never summarise the important incidents in your stories: always give them directly.

There are probably as many ways of writing dialogue as there are writers. Dialogue can be quite stylised, yet very effective, as in Russell Hoban's books for young readers. *Dinner at Alberta's* is an amusing one to have a look at, as is *The Owl who was Afraid of the Dark* by Jill

Tomlinson. In longer stories the dialogue will probably be less rhythmic and more 'natural' sounding than in the above examples – more as people commonly do speak. Yet writing dialogue is really a technique as well. It is *not* simply a matter of rushing around behind children with a tape-recorder in order to be able to produce authentic-sounding conversation. Indeed if writers *did* render what children actually do say, and the way in which they say it, I think child readers (and everybody else) would be very bored. It is true, however, that you do have to break up what your characters say, and make them repeat things, as people do all the time in life. In other words, don't write long speeches and call it conversation.

Determining what to put in dialogue and what to put in summary form is one of the great problems for the beginning writer. Just remember that dialogue should always be a high point, as we noted in picture books, and you will be able to resist the temptation to give information about your plot or characters or setting in dialogue form when it could be presented more succinctly or credibly in other ways. Dialogue should always convey character. The best writers are those who manage to distinguish their characters not only by what they say but by how they say it. Writers who manage to do this are E. B. White in *Charlotte's Web*, A. A. Milne in *Winnie-the-Pooh* and Jan Mark in all her titles. It is well worth taking the time to study what these writers do. I shall be looking in more detail at dialogue in Chapter 6.

It's really all a question then of taking an idea and developing it through situation and character, through description and dialogue. It is important, also, to think of situation and character together. It is really difficult

to try to imagine your character in a vacuum;
fortunately, you don't have to. Put your character in a
particular situation and you will start to see how he or
she will react. In a sense characters in fiction are fake:
they only exist within particular contexts. Take them
out of these situations and contexts and they will
collapse. So, you don't have to create a convincing
character as such. What you do have to do is make your
creation function credibly in one particular scene and
then consistently in the next scene, and so on. When I
realised this, I felt much more comfortable about
character creation. And don't worry if you have
difficulty at the beginning in expanding ideas
appropriately. Most people do have trouble, I'm sure.
What I do believe is that you can learn to do this by
practising your writing and by studying good models.

TRY THIS!

- Take an idea for a story and write it up in varying lengths. Try
  50 words
  500 words
  1000 words

- Write your own animal story, of at least 2000 words.

  You may just have written a book!
  (An Omnibus Dipper title, as you may remember, is 1500 to 2500 words, and 2000-2500 words is the lower limit of a Young Puffin.)

CHAPTER 5

Novels and Short Stories (11+ Years)
The Organisation of Your Story

MAKING A START

This is the terrifying part for beginning writers: we long to write a novel, but where on earth do we start? Actually you can start anywhere, with a title, a character, a situation, even an image. It will probably be something unusual that will attract your attention initially. Just as our eyes are attuned to register movement, so do our writers' eyes tend to be alerted for anything unusual or incongruous in our environment. And I think that this is probably the secret of making a start. We don't want to write about what is usual and ordinary; if we pick something that is unusual, above all, something that is *puzzling*, we have made a head start, for our readers are sure to be interested if we are puzzled by our material too.

Charles Dickens apparently worked on his novels like this: he would divide a sheet of paper up into two, and put all the questions he had of his story on the left. Then he would try gradually to fill in the answers on the right. *Why has she done that? Why would he have come to the town just at this point? Does she really care about her daughter at all?* These would be the kinds of questions that he would ask of himself.

What readers and prospective writers sometimes don't realise is that writers often don't know either why their characters have done certain things. They too are faced with particular actions and then have to work out explanations for them. Writers who aren't quite sure what their characters will do next may well be the most interesting ones, for they are really creating characters who have the capacity to surprise, even to surprise their creator. If a writer seems to know his (or her) characters all round there can be something very predictable about the stories. You feel as if you know in advance how the characters will act and react. It is almost as if the author is a little bit bored with the characters, perhaps doesn't even like them very much, and of course this is passed on to the reader.

You may find this a strange concept: the idea of writers not knowing everything about their characters. After all, they have created them, you might argue. But characters, once created, often behave in quite unexpected ways. Suppose you visualise a scene really vividly, and then write it up (usually a bit less vividly!). But in the scene the character behaves in a way that does not appear to be consistent with his behaviour elsewhere. You then either have to cut the scene or else use it to explore some unexpected dimension in the character.

But, you might be wondering, how am I going to find an idea that can be developed at novel length? Don't worry. If you have been writing every day and turning your thoughts consciously towards the making of stories, the idea will find you. At the moment I am haunted by an image: it is an image I found in John Mortimer's autobiography *Clinging to the Wreckage*. It is simply the image of a woman cleaning out a telephone box. In the autobiography the explanation is simply that she is a terribly clean woman who has run out of objects to wash at home. But what if this weren't the reason? Perhaps the phone box was to be a meeting place or she was expecting a secret call there. She may have wanted to observe what was going on in the opposite house or give the impression that she was eccentric – and harmless. Perhaps she wanted to distract attention away from her own house where something strange really was going on. She may have wanted to provide herself with an alibi. Perhaps she was running away from her children and wanted the peace of the phone box to write a novel in!

Now even if this idea ever came to anything, I shouldn't think it would resolve itself into a novel, although I suppose it is possible that it could. At first, anyway, I thought there might be a picture book idea in there somewhere, or else a short story for younger children. It would all depend on how the idea developed. And this brings me to the next point: ideas have a habit, fortunately and helpfully, of developing on their own. You are all familiar with the phenomenon of going to bed with a problem unsolved, sleeping perfectly, and then waking up with the solution. Somehow your mind has been working away at the problem even when you were unaware of this. It's like that with stories. If you file an idea away in your head somewhere, it may well pop out days or months or even years later, almost fully formed. With a novel, you do need time for the germ of it to develop. You will find that all sorts of apparently extraneous material will start to get dragged into it, without conscious effort on your part.

What you want are *puzzles*. Often situations in life will hand you these on a platter. I was having lunch once at home with an extremely able student of mine, Janie Williams. We were discussing the very promising opening chapters of a novel she had embarked on. I started to tell her about a recent experience of ours, at home. My son had asked me one weekend if I had seen his money-box, but I hadn't. Then my daughter looked for hers. It wasn't there either. So I looked in a drawer and found that my foreign money had gone out of an old purse. We looked all round the house and found a door open which normally is always kept locked. Then we discovered the money-boxes, emptied out in a far corner of the garden with a trail of small money leading up to the road.

You can see that we are not a very observant family, as it had taken us several days to notice that we had been robbed. But it wasn't *just* that we'd been unobservant. What seemed strange was that there was no sign of disturbance: no opened drawers, nothing. Looking back, all I could remember that had been unusual was that on the Tuesday or Wednesday when I had come home I had noticed that the dog was shut up in our bedroom. That *had* seemed odd as she always has the run of the house, but at the time I just thought that my husband had absent-mindedly shut the door after him. She was favouring a leg, though, almost as if she'd been kicked . . .

To me this was all a puzzle, and my mind brooded over it for some time. It seemed clear that it was a gang of children who were involved for they hadn't taken anything except the money. Children of about twelve, I

thought, for all my son's Stephen King novels had
disappeared too. A literary gang, then. They had left
nothing disturbed: no sign at all. A tidy gang – perhaps
there was a girl in it, I thought (in no doubt a sexist
way!). And then there was the dog. That really *was* a
puzzle, for we all knew that the dog would have barked
her head off – and yet they had still come in and then
shut her away in a room.

And I think at that point I got the idea for my story.
It posed itself as a question: what if the dog *hadn't*
barked, at least until they got in? Under what possible
circumstances would the dog not have barked? And
when I solved that one, I was well on the way to having
not only the start but the main direction of my story.

I told all this to Janie who listened with polite interest
as perhaps you are doing now. When I had finished she
said rather gloomily, 'It's a novel you're thinking about.
You do see that, don't you?' She said it gloomily because
she was having terrible trouble in forcing her novel to
move away from its opening scene on a surfing beach
and probably wanted to save me from similar agony.
After all she knew that I was perfectly happy writing
short, more manageable stories for children.

I stared at her, knowing it was true, and feeling as if I
were standing at the edge of a freezing sea. I knew also,
quite clearly, that I didn't want to step in, didn't want to
attempt a novel, not yet anyway. It was too early, I was
too inexperienced, I didn't have the time, I was
working, my daughter was about to start her last, so
important, year at school. It was quite simply the wrong
time. But even as I argued with myself I could feel the
idea of the story pulling me in.

The same thing will happen to you if you dabble
around in stories. One day you will get an idea that

cannot possibly resolve itself within a few pages: an idea that you will simply have to develop. Give yourself plenty of time and the idea almost of itself will appear to grow.

MODELS

We learn to write by writing and we also learn to write by studying good models. Fortunately there are plenty of excellent models in this area of children's books; indeed I think it would be fair to say that this is the richest category of all for quality titles. Here we have the writers of early in the century like Edith Nesbit and Frances Hodgson Burnett; writers of the thirties like J. R. R. Tolkien and Arthur Ransome; writers starting their careers in the fifties like Lucy Boston, Philippa Pearce, C. S. Lewis, Mary Norton and William Mayne in England, and Patricia Wrightson, Joan Phipson, Ivan Southall and Eleanor Spence in Australia; writers of the sixties like Leon Garfield and Alan Garner; writers of the seventies like Jane Gardam, Jan Mark and Katherine Paterson; writers of the eighties like Janni Howker and Cynthia Voigt and, in Australia, Gillian Rubinstein, Robin Klein, Victor Kelleher and Caroline Macdonald. So what I want us now to do is look at various openings to children's books which suggest what the key to each particular story was: was it a character, a situation, situation *and* character, an image or a particular narrator voice that came to the writer as the best way in to the story? First let's look at getting into a story through a character.

Character

One of the best-loved stories of the twentieth century must surely be *The Secret Garden* by Frances Hodgson Burnett. Published in 1911 it remains a steady seller today. There must be many reasons for its appeal, but one of the most important of these is the depiction of the character Mary Lennox in the opening paragraph of the novel:

When Mary Lennox was sent to Misselthwaite Manor to live with her uncle, everybody said she was the most disagreeable-looking child ever seen. It was true, too. She had a little thin face and a little thin body, thin light hair and a sour expression. Her hair was yellow, and her face was yellow because she had been born in India and had always been ill in one way or another.

You might well wonder why a disagreeable-looking, plain, sickly child should appeal to children who are never very patient with illness. Later in the same paragraph we learn that she not only *looks* disagreeable, for 'by the time she was six years old she was as tyrannical and selfish a little pig as ever lived'. But appeal she certainly does. Perhaps this is because she creates a feeling of relief, even of release, in children. They know that they are often thought to be disagreeable too, and to see someone depicted as the heroine, although worse than they are, makes them feel better. There is also nothing to envy here; they are put in a position where they can pity, and hence feel superior to Mary, trapped as she is by her situation and by her unpleasant personality. Her lack of health and her bad temper are, of course, very important to the plot, for we are to find that under the influence of various gardens Mary is to change and blossom.

Erica Yurken is another character who interests her readers straight away:

I will never forgive my mother for calling me Erica with a surname like Yurken.

When an emergency teacher was taking our grade (we got a lot of emergency teachers at our school because the ordinary ones were often away with nervous problems), the emergency teacher would say something like, 'Girl in the end row with the dark hair, what's your name?' But before I could answer, kids would screech out 'Erk!' Or 'Yuk!' Or 'Gherkin!' Except Barry Hollis who always yelled out something worse, but emergency teachers were given a counselling session by the Principal before they came into our room, so they knew enough to pretend not to hear Barry Hollis.

This passage comes from the opening page of Robin Klein's very popular *Hating Alison Ashley*.

I think that this kind of writing appeals to children because it imitates the racy, cheery, rather cheeky way in which they see themselves as thinking and performing at school, or at least it gives an exaggerated, a glamorised image of this kind of activity. The first-person form is also a very direct, a very involving one for young readers. At once they are well within the thought stream of someone they like to see as being very similar to themselves.

Even in this short passage the vitality and humour of the character are clear. Indeed so full of energy is this character that she shares the spotlight of the story on at least an equal basis with the character who has been put in central focus: Alison Ashley herself. This doesn't happen often. I have only ever used the first-person narrative once, in *A Lamb Like Alice*, a story for younger readers. I intended the main protagonist to be the narrator, the 'I' of the story, not realising that it is the person the narrator focuses on who will, very often, become the central character. I meant this to be Sophie, the child who tells the story, but alas, it turned out to be Dan. And he, after all, is more interesting – mischievous, quirky, inventive and warm-hearted. But it happened mainly, I think, because of point of view. The first-person narrator tends just to become a means of mediating the story unless you take a lot of care.

Plot

The following extract comes from the second page of Paul Jennings's story 'Pink Bow Tie', the first in his collection *Unbelievable!*. Each of his stories contains a mystery to which we are alerted early; we then read helplessly on to see how it will be resolved. His ideas are not ordinary ones and belong more to the realm of nightmares and strange dreams than to the everyday world, although they are firmly rooted in it. The boy of the first story has just started at a new school; of the second is having a tooth filled; of the third has had his grandfather put away in a home; of the fourth has just come home with a video cassette entitled 'Chainsaw Murder', and so on. In this first story the author's 'hook' is the colour of the boy's hair. The boy has been summoned in by the headmaster:

'Well, lad,' says Old Splodge. 'Why have you dyed your hair? Trying to be a surfie, eh?' He is a grumpy old boy. He is due to retire next year and he does not want to go.

I notice that he is still wearing the pink bow tie. He always wears this bow tie. He cannot seem to live without it. I try not to look at it as I answer him. 'I did not dye my hair, sir,' I say.

'Yesterday,' says Splodge, 'when I gave you six of the best, I noticed that you had black hair. Am I correct?'

'Yes, sir,' I answer.

'Then tell me, lad,' he says. 'How is it that your hair is white today?' I notice that little purple veins are standing out on his bald head. This is a bad sign.

'It's a long story,' I tell him.

'Tell me the long story,' he says. 'And it had better be good.'

We too want to hear 'the long story', knowing that in Paul Jennings's hands it *will* be good.

Here we have a plot based on an apparent contradiction: the boy's hair has changed from black to white but has not been dyed, so we read on to see how this can possibly be resolved. In the passage some of the information which appears to be only incidental is, in fact, crucial: the fact that the headmaster always wears a pink bow tie, for example, and that he doesn't want to retire. There is also a red herring: ' "Trying to be a surfie, eh?" ' Notice too how he keys off the dialogue – the second speaker takes up what the first speaker says and develops it to humorous effect: ' "It's a long story," ' . . . "Tell me the long story," ' . . . There are also frequent laconic, understated touches: 'This is a bad sign', the narrator informs us.

Plot is more important than character in Paul Jennings's stories. The stories are mostly told in the first person and the narrator is of little interest in each case: just a window on to the story. His characters tend to be shadowy beings, performing their parts in exaggerated, caricatured ways for the sake of the situation in which they find themselves. I think of him as a kind of

Australian equivalent of Roald Dahl. He is the sort of writer that many children, who are not particularly readers, are likely to respond to, for he combines strong story-telling skills with a simple, very direct and most distinctive style.

Victor Kelleher is another Australian author (for a slightly older age group) who also possesses strong story-telling skills, deals in puzzles, and has a simple, direct style. What follows is the passage from his novel *Del-Del* where Beth first becomes aware of a very real change in her brother:

I expected to find him curled up amongst his jumpers and spare blankets. Not crying, because he never cried, but at least looking sorry for himself. Instead, he was sitting cross-legged at the back of the cupboard, dry-eyed and calm, staring at me. His face, like the rest of the room, was somehow changed. Not physically. He was still the same skinny little kid as before, but with something different about him. And I mean really different, like looking at someone you think you know and seeing a stranger. Someone who shouldn't be there.

Notice how he expands, elaborates on his sentences so that the passage has a cohesive effect and gives you a sense of somebody actually thinking: 'different . . . really different; someone . . . Someone who shouldn't be there'.

Plot and character
And what would you think of a novel which begins like this?

In those days I had never given a thought to poisoning and I can be sure of this, that I had nothing to do with our mother's death.

This seems to me to be a sure-fire opening sentence. It tells you straight away that the plot will hinge on murders, and that, although a first-person viewpoint, you are entering an abnormal psychology. I say 'although' because the first-person viewpoint is a very persuasive one, and it usually needs a lot of contrary evidence to make us disbelieve in it. Not so here.

The sentence raises many questions: who is this person with the distorted view on life? Why has she now 'given a thought to poisoning'? What has happened to change her? (Somehow the speaker sounds to me as if it is a woman or girl. Perhaps it is simply that I have read further, or perhaps I get that impression because it *is* often women who turn to poisoning as a means of causing death, and somehow too because of the use of the word 'our'. I think a man or boy would have used the more personal 'my' – 'my mother's death'. The 'our' is at once more precise and colder, more impersonal.) There also seems to be something strange about the 'I can be sure of this . . .' for it implies that she *isn't* sure about her involvement in other deaths, presumably from poisoning. The sentence even suggests that *emotionally*, at least, it would have been perfectly possible for her to have had something to do with her mother's death, although in *fact* she hasn't. 'In those days' also has a particular effect. The story presumably won't be about 'those days', the days of comparative innocence. It makes you shudder when you wonder what 'these days' are going to be like.

This is only the opening sentence and yet it suggests all this; the spring of the story is coiled up in so few words. The reader at once feels interested in the plot and in the strange psychology that is about to mediate the story for us, no doubt through a distorted perspective.

Much of the interest of the novel will in fact derive from trying to assess just how far events and characters *are* being distorted by the viewpoint of the narrator.

The author is Ruth Rendell, who sometimes writes under the name of Barbara Vine when she feels that she is writing more of a novel and less of a mystery. She has written many fascinating and chilling murder-mysteries including *A Dark-Adapted Eye*, *Living Flesh*, *A Fatal Inversion* and this novella, *Heartstones*. The point of view of this short novel is that of a teenage anorexic girl, and because of this, and the length, the book could well have been published as adolescent fiction. However, and perhaps because all her other books have been produced as thrillers for adults, this one has been marketed in the same way.

What follows is the opening passage of another first-person novel (this time marketed for the 11+ age group) which excites our interest in both the narrator and the plot:

February 6

I don't know what I am doing here.
Well, I do really. It's because I was getting nowhere at
the Hospital. I have been sent here to learn to talk again.
Sent here because my mother can't stand my silent
presence at home. Sent here because of my face, I
suppose. I don't know.

The extract is from John Marsden's *So Much to Tell You* . . . You will notice that it, too, presupposes a lot about what has happened in the past: her stay in hospital, her deteriorating relationship with her mother, some problem with her face. We, as readers, find ourselves asking several questions: Why does the speaker have to learn to talk again? What kind of hospital has she been in and why? Why doesn't she talk to her mother? What has happened to her face? We are aware too of the confusion of the narrator: 'I don't know', she begins, then 'Well, I do really', and then back to the 'I don't know' at the end of the passage.

Image
Badger on the Barge could be enjoyed by a sensitive twelve-year-old perhaps, but most people reading the stories would be older than that. It is Janni Howker's first book and as such, is quite remarkable. It is a collection of stories each of which features some aspect of the relationship between old and young. The following extract is from the first and title story:

October smelled of bonfires, even in Alfred Street. Down by the canal the yellow leaves of the big conker trees flickered and rustled like burning newspapers. In the still canal water black leaves floated on Helen's reflection.

"Come ye thankful people, come,
Raise the song of harvest home.
All is safely gathered in
'Ere the winter storms begin . . . " she sang softly. Across the canal she could see King Alfred's Grammar School, high and holy on its hill above the empty cricket-field. Peter didn't go there any more.

At first the passage seems to be simply descriptive, although the description is interesting and unusual. It is October, bonfire time, but notice how this is expressed: 'October smelled of bonfires . . .' Then there seems to be something strange about the next word, 'even': 'even in Alfred Street'. Why is Alfred Street being singled out, we might ask? What is different about Alfred Street? Why shouldn't it be having a bonfire like everywhere else?

The images of autumn don't seem to be entirely pleasant either. The 'yellow leaves' are all right, but the image of them rustling and flickering 'like burning newspapers' is not exactly a pretty one. The uneasiness which this image creates is increased by the next one: 'In the still canal water black leaves floated on Helen's reflection'. It is as if Helen is being blotted out by the black leaves, by the burning autumn. Even the harvest hymn creates the dual effect – of reassurance but of anxiety too in the part of the song which Helen sings under her breath: ''Ere the winter storms begin . . . '

For some reason Helen is clearly against King Alfred's Grammar School: she resents it, 'high and holy on its hill'. And the passage ends with a rather desolate image, the 'empty' cricket-field, followed by the short, unelaborated sentence (equally desolate) 'Peter didn't go there any more'.

Of course Peter may simply have changed schools, been expelled, gone to another town or grown up, but somehow the rest of the passage seems to have been building up to this stark sentence. We try to think of other reasons, but at the same time the attentive reader probably guesses that Peter is, in fact, dead.

The autumn images have already suggested this, as has the subdued quality of the words chosen: words that suggest slight movement or none at all, like 'flickered', 'floated' and 'still'; words that suggest slight sound like 'rustled' and 'softly', and negative words, denoting absence of quality, like 'black' and 'empty'.

The effect then is a cumulative one; the images are predominantly suggestive of desolation, of emptiness. Note too, that you aren't told who Helen is, or Peter, or what the relationship is between them. An opening page should raise questions, not provide answers. The writer wants you to read on.

Always take a lot for granted when you start a story – don't feel that you have to explain who everybody is or what they look like. First arouse interest in your characters, in their situation. There will be plenty of time later to fill in the details about them. It can be very off-putting at the beginning of a story to be given too much information about characters before you have had a chance to become really involved with them. Try not to explain too much. We are in the business, remember, of puzzles and mysteries.

Which reminds me of my lady cleaning out the telephone box. Maybe she thinks she is wiping away the evidence? Perhaps it was the scene of a crime, but long ago? She still worries me, incessantly washing the floor, cleaning the phone, rearranging the telephone book.

Narrator voice
Let's turn to something more cheerful now, and look at the effect of narrator voice in persuading us to read on. The following extract comes from the opening page of Penelope Lively's delightful collection of stories, *A House Inside Out*. The house is 'inside out' because we are looking at it from the point of view of the creatures who live within it and around it: creatures like the pigeons, the mice, the dog, wood-lice and spiders, who, in their own way, own the house.

Dogs are odd. They are animals, no doubt about that; but to other animals they often seem like offshoots of human beings. This was certainly true of the dog at Fifty-four Pavilion Road, a rough-haired white terrier

called Willie. The other creatures in the house thought
Willie a helpless fellow because he depended on the
Dixon family for food and a roof over his head. Mind, in
the case of the mice this could have been said of them
also, but I suppose they would have retorted that at least
they risked life and limb to get their meals whereas
Willie had his handed to him in a bowl. But the real
difference is one of outlook rather than the getting of
food and shelter. Dogs tend to take a human point of
view; they even behave, up to a point, like people.

Willie loved Mrs. Dixon. In fact, he didn't just love
Mrs. Dixon – he adored and worshipped her. He was
polite to the rest of the family, but it was Mrs. Dixon
who was the centre of his world.

Penelope Lively has somehow managed to capture the
tone of the speaking voice. It's partly a matter of how
she structures her sentences. Sentences and phrases like
'Dogs are odd', 'This was certainly true', 'Mind', and
'but I suppose', all give you in their directness and
colloquial nature, not to mention the use of the first
person, the sense that you are being spoken to. Notice
how the author builds on previous sentences: to expand,
to qualify what has been said, and simply, to create a
prose which is cohesive. An example of this would be
the opening three sentences of the second paragraph,
'Willie loved Mrs. Dixon', and onwards. The writer
takes the first simple sentence and then qualifies it,
intensifying Willie's feeling for comic effect. Nor does
she leave it at that for we have a third sentence,
heightening the effect still more by telling us that it is
Mrs Dixon who is at the centre of Willie's small world.

This passage, then, establishes a feeling of closeness
between author and reader as well as creating a very

warm character in Willie. In the second paragraph, as you will have noticed, Penelope Lively moves into the viewpoint of Willie and we see things from now on, often humorously, through his perspective. Mrs Dixon, we learn, is also very fond of Willie, but she frequently complains that he gets underfoot so that she is constantly falling over him. ' "It's not me that's underfoot," Willie would grumble, "it's you who are overdog." '

BEGINNINGS

We have now looked at getting into a story in various ways: through character, plot, plot and character simultaneously, through image and finally through a narrator voice that establishes a very strong link between author and reader. Don't think, though, that beginnings are always written first in a story; and even if they are, they are likely to go through several upheavals and modifications before the story is finished. As you can see, the beginning of a story must furnish reliable clues both as to the kind of story it is and how it is to be conducted. It is likely to be very packed, very concentrated, because of these requirements.

It should also sound as though you are coming in on the middle of a scene: it's as if you enter a room and the characters are already there, already talking. It's not the beginning for them, the characters. It is as if you are eavesdropping on them at a particularly interesting stage in their lives. The impression you want to create is that they have existed before, without you, and will again after this story is over.

Try to notice in your own reading how stories begin

and you will see at once what I mean. Here are a couple
of excellent examples, the first one from Anne Fine's
unusual novel *The Granny Project*:

*The doctor was having a hard time in the Harris family.
He'd been around to their house often enough before, of
course. He'd been their family doctor for years. He'd seen
them bellowing red-faced in cots, or miserably picking at
their chicken poxes, or coughing horribly in steamed-up bath-
rooms. He'd never seen them all together in one room, and
well, before. The noise was appalling. The four of them, two
girls, two boys, sat round the kitchen table eating like wolves.
There was much scraping of knives and grating of forks. All
the plates rattled on the table top. They were, the doctor
realised after a moment's perplexed reflection, all seconds,
warped in the kiln and sold off cheaply in the market.*

The second passage is from the title story of Jan
Mark's model collection, *Nothing to be Afraid Of*:

*'Robin won't give you any trouble,' said Auntie Lynn.
'He's very quiet.'*
    *Anthea knew how quiet Robin was. At present he
was sitting under the table and, until Auntie Lynn
mentioned his name, she had forgotten that he was
there.*
    Auntie Lynn put a carrier bag on the armchair.
    *'There's plenty of clothes, so you won't need to do any
washing, and there's a spare pair of pyjamas in case –
well, you know. In case . . .'*
    *'Yes,' said Mum, firmly. 'He'll be all right. I'll ring
you tonight and let you know how he's getting along.'
She looked at the clock. 'Now, hadn't you better be
getting along?'*

In 1987 I gave my writing class the following
exercise: they were to write the opening paragraph of a
first-person narrative – 'just ten minutes,' I said. You
will be interested to know that most of them went on to
complete the story thus begun:

1. *It isn't fair. It just isn't. My mother says it never is at my age.
For once she's right. I bet I'm the only person I know, probably
the only person in the whole world, who's not allowed to walk to
school alone. It's embarrassing having to walk with your mother.
I always walk a few steps in front of her, but still, everyone knows.*

2. *Well, that's it. My life is over. No point in ever going back
to school. To think, just last week I thought I was actually going
to like the new school!*

3. *She was a revolting girl. Her hair was messy, her dress was
dirty and she smelt funny. Nobody at school liked her and she
didn't deserve to have any friends. When she headed towards me I
thought, oh no, go away.*

4. *Why do I always get blamed for everything? If something
goes missing I get blamed. If a kid gets hit I get blamed. Why
won't anyone believe me when I tell the truth?*

5. *I told him that we were too young, that it couldn't be done.
THAT I DIDN'T WANT TO!!
Besides, I was sure Mum and Dad had other ideas.*

6. *I was becoming more and more frustrated, but I wasn't ready
to give up. With one foot balanced either side of the mast, I took
hold of the thick rope in both hands and heaved. Slowly,
painfully, the mast rose out of the water, and the brand new sail
flapped impatiently in front of me.*

I thought then, and still think now, that these are extraordinarily good. In the first one, it is the expansions which are particularly effective: 'I'm the only person . . . probably the only person . . .' and the 'but still, everyone knows', with its world-weary tone, rounds off the passage nicely.

The exaggeration of the second passage really makes you want to read on to find out whatever happened at the new school, while the third passage arouses your interest in the repulsive character and makes you wonder about the speaker. Is he too fastidious? Surely he is exaggerating about the girl? He does seem very hard with his, 'and she didn't deserve to have any friends'. The fourth opening is more ordinary, but you could imagine a child identifying with all of that and wanting to read on.

The fifth passage is rather fascinating, isn't it? It raises so many questions. You wonder what on earth the children are up to: what are they too young for, and why can't they do it, whatever it is? In what way do the mother and father have other ideas? I think this one is interesting because the sentences seem to be full of contradictory propositions. We wonder what can reconcile them all.

The last passage is slower, more descriptive, and indeed turned out to be introducing an idea which would need the slow, gradual development of the novel form.

I find that my classes have less difficulty with the first-person narrative form, perhaps because they are still so young themselves that they can readily identify with the voice of a child just a few years younger. It is also, of course, the most direct form of story-telling.

DEVELOPING YOUR STORY

Uncomfortable situations

As we were saying earlier, give your story-idea a chance to grow. The mistake most beginning writers make is to put too much material in. They don't know how to fill out the frightening 150 or so blank sheets of the novel form (about 50,000 words plus) and so they keep adding material. 'Be mean with your ideas,' a writer friend once said to me, and it is true: make one small idea last out for a whole novel.

As I mentioned before (in Chapter 3), put your main character in an uncomfortable position and then prevent him from getting out of it too easily. Don't make it too easy for your character *or for yourself* to find a resolution. Your protagonist will be impeded by a host of things, the size of the difficulty increasing all the time up to the climax of the story. He may be impeded by circumstances, by another character perhaps, and, most powerfully of all, by his own nature. It is always helpful if someone is somehow *against* your character and opposed to his achieving his goal. You then have a strong focus for conflict; the stronger the characters, the more intense the conflict. An opposing character like this provides a focus for the frustrated feelings of the protagonist and the reader. And plotting has a lot to do with the creation of feelings of frustration in the reader. When you watch a soapie, notice how close the protagonist comes to achieving his goal time after time (like winning the love of the beautiful girl), but some obstacle always appears at the last minute. The reader longs for the frustration to end, but when it does, of course, so does the story.

See if you can identify the uncomfortable situation in

the books that you are reading. In Jan Mark's *Thunder and Lightnings* Andrew's family shift to Norfolk and he has to make a new start at a rather unpromising new school. I suppose we then feel that once he makes a friend he will be comfortable again. Or there is Erica Yurken in *Hating Alison Ashley*, who is envious of another girl, but without admitting it, even to herself, she really admires her and wants to be her friend. Frances is the teenage protagonist in Robin Klein's powerful *People Might Hear You*. Her aunt marries into a strange religious sect and her whole way of life is overturned. Then, in Gillian Rubinstein's *Space Demons*, there is the twelve-year-old, Andrew, who is bored by everything and becomes unhealthily obsessed with a computer game. In *The Broken Saddle* by James Aldridge a child falls in love with a pony because it *is* wild, but is then persuaded to tame it. Jan Mark's *At the Sign of the Dog and Rocket* is about a teenager trying to run a hotel almost on her own after her father is injured. In Robert Cormier's *The Bumblebee Flies Anyway* a boy is being used, unknowingly, for psychological experiments in a hospital for terminally ill children. A boy is haunted by a poltergeist in Penelope Lively's *The Ghost of Thomas Kempe*, and in another novel of hers, *The House in Norham Gardens*, a young girl is terrified that her ancient aunts will die and leave her alone in a huge, echoing Victorian house. In Jane Gardam's *Bilgewater* a girl is so perceptive that people outside the family think that she is a bit mad. In 'The Egg Man' by Janni Howker a child is approached by an old, peculiar man, and has difficulty in explaining to her parents the experience she has had. In 'Wunderpants' by Paul Jennings the narrator is caught, miles from home, without any clothes. And we could make up plenty of our own. What about a child whose parents set her impossible goals? Or a family who are so wrapped up in their sick child that they neglect the healthy one? Or a brother and sister who get on perfectly together until they learn that one of them is adopted? Or a child whose fascination with a strange woman whose activities include washing out the local telephone box leads him into danger??

Forms of repetition
Try and think of ways to hold your story together – to give it unity and cohesion, and to help the fabric of it all to stay in the reader's mind. You may want to use images to bind it, as Janni Howker does in *Badger on the Barge*. You may wish to use some other form of repetition: repeating a phrase, or an action or a thought, or perhaps all of these.

A story often doesn't shape itself in a simply linear way at all, but in a series of connected, advancing loops, each looping section to do with some repeated action. This action or thought will prepare for and build up to the climax of the novel. You will find that many novels will hover around one particular event or image: Robert Westall's *The Scarecrows* on the three scarecrows in the field beside Simon's house; Jane Gardam's *The Summer After the Funeral* on the graveyard where Athene's father lies buried; Penelope Lively's *The House in Norham Gardens* on the image of snow.

In *The House Guest* I made the action keep returning to the room in the house that is always shut: the room that belongs to Hugh but who is never there. This last suggests to the reader that the climax of the action will concern itself with a meeting between the protagonist and this other mysterious boy.

Each time when the action returns to the same point the repetitions will be modified, often intensifying as

you approach the climax which these are, in effect,
preparing the reader for. It's like playing on a theme, as
if it were music. The 'loop' sections will often be
chapter endings, thereby drawing attention to what you
are repeating, and at the same time helping to pull the
reader from one chapter into the next.

In *The House Guest*, Chapter 2 ends with Hugh's
room:

What was wrong with the room was its
smell: the room smelt musty, unused, as if no one ever
came into it.

And Chapter 5 ends with Hugh himself:

It was only when he was in bed that night that he realised
what the poem had made him think of – or rather, who
it made him think of. The poem made him think of
Hugh.

Chapter 6 ends in this way:

Or if he could have gone to the cemetery with Hugh . . .
One thing sure about that, even if it had been possible, there
would have been no point in drawing Hugh's attention
to the spelling of the sign.

At the end of Chapter 8 Gunno is examining a
photograph which he has found in Hugh's room:

The picture then was just of trees, just of trees
growing out of a high form of scrub. Only of trees, and
yet, as Gunno stared at it, he felt a tingle of unease, and
shivered a little as if he were cold.

These endings help to turn the story in the direction of Hugh, so that the reader will wonder about him too. Once the story becomes a straightforward quest to find him, there is no need for the looping device and the story can move on in a more linear way to its climax.

The climax
You have to prepare then, very carefully (throughout your story), for the climax. Indeed the seeds of it should probably even be in your opening page, if possible. The climax of the novel must always be given in detail; it must be visualised directly, never summarised. It should be in some way crucial for the protagonist: things will never be the same again afterwards, whatever happens. Its outcome shouldn't be obvious, otherwise there will be insufficient tension at the heart of your story. It should be possible for events to go really badly or to turn out well.

I would suggest too that you write your climax early, as soon as you can even partly visualise it. I have found that beginning writers often skip the climax. By the time they get to it they are so exhausted that they simply summarise events in a few dead paragraphs, and then, with great relief, wind up the story. Sometimes they even miss it out all together, letting the idea of it trickle away sadly in the space between two other chapters. It may come as a relief to you to know that a story doesn't need to be written in its final order. Indeed it seems wise to write up a scene that we can imagine clearly, especially if we are feeling excited about it, whether it comes at the end or middle or wherever of the story. We must discipline ourselves to write even when we don't feel like it, but if we do then let's take advantage of it. Some writers, but by no means all, do write steadily through their stories, but others jump around. Philippa Pearce, for example, imagined the magnificent ending to her novel *A Dog So Small* almost first, and Gillian Rubinstein always does her main scenes at the beginning, filling in the bridging passages afterwards.

I felt appalled by the whole idea of writing a novel as I had always only written short pieces, but when I found that you could write bits here and there, as if you were filling in a jigsaw, I felt much happier about it. And really, in the end, it doesn't seem to matter if you do it this way – the parts all join up together quite miraculously. Emotionally it seems much easier as it does away with the frightening feeling of having to somehow get from A to B.

Writers like Robert Cormier and Robert Westall are particularly good at generating suspense, and the climaxes of their novels are worth studying. The scarecrows in the novel of that name by Robert Westall are endowed with a sinister form of life. Here, at the climax of the novel, Simon has to run through the field that harbours them in order to reach the old mill:

"Run, Simon, run!"
Run, Simon, run. *Like on the rugby-field. All the kids, all the masters shouting, and the ball in his hands.*

He ran. Smashed through the hedge as if it was a rugby-pack. Felt the branches clutch at his shirt and tear away despairingly.

He darted between the figures of the scarecrows. Starkey was still lurking at the back. He almost ran into him, into the filthy smell of rotting straw; but swerved just in time. The turnip-leaves, full of rain, lashed his ankles like whips and threw wet up his trousers. He trampled on the rounded bodies of the turnips as if he was in a black room full of hard solid rugby-balls . . .

He was panting now; great gouts of breath. Panting in total darkness, but still running, running for the mill. And somehow he knew, in all that turnip-filled darkness, just exactly where the mill was. If he was tied beyond hope to the mill, the mill was also tied beyond hope to him. It couldn't escape him, no more than he could escape it.

Simon's father is dead and his mother has remarried. His fierce loyalty to his dead father results in a growing and bitter conflict between him and his (at first) easy-going stepfather. The scarecrows become a visible expression of his hatred, a hatred that is now rebounding upon himself. Robert Westall knows how to keep his readers with him, right up to the last pages. This extract is taken from page 155 of a 160 page novel.

Note how he punctuates the passage and abbreviates in order to keep up the pace: 'He ran. Smashed . . . Felt . . .' More usually you might say: 'He ran, smashing through . . . feeling . . .' but the participles lack the strength of the past tense. The passage has a staccato effect, particularly in the first half, to give this impression of speed. The image of the rugby field unifies the passage and helps give it its frantic quality. Even the turnips become rugby balls and all his movements are associated with the game – he *smashed* through the hedge, *darted* between the figures of the scarecrows and *swerved* just in time. The environment is hostile: the branches *clutch* at his shirt, the scarecrow is *lurking*, and the turnip leaves lash his ankles *like whips*.

The words used throughout the passage suggest nightmare, suggest the distortion which Simon's state of mind is giving to ordinary events and objects. The passage ends more quietly, but in such a way that the reader will want to read on to find out what happens next:

*If he was tied beyond hope to the mill, the mill was
also tied beyond hope to him. It couldn't escape him, no more
than he could escape it.*

    This careful balancing of the mill and Simon is what
slows the passage down and brings it to a quiet finish.

ENDINGS

We have noted that the climax came only five pages
before the completion of *The Scarecrows*, and really I
think it would be correct to say that in most cases the
climax is the true ending of a novel. The chapters or
pages which follow are usually only concerned with
rounding off the action, whose main interest has now
disappeared with the resolution of the conflict. A story,
then, usually has two endings, and it is important to get
them both right. Quite a lot of writers seem to lose
interest in their story and don't bother with the
rounding off that the reader really needs. You know
yourself if you have been totally involved in a story you
need to be let down gradually. There needs to be a slow
falling away at the end where you are reassured about
the fate of the characters and where any loose ends are
tied up. As a writer you want to make this part as
interesting as you can, not making it sound like a dose of
terminal information.

    A sense of the ending should somehow be present in
your beginning and a remembrance of the beginning
should haunt your ending. Your true ending will be the
highest point of the action; the opening chapter may
well be the second highest point.

Don't cheat your reader either in the chapters after the climax. If it has been a sad book with a sad climax don't try to make it as if nothing has happened at all just for the sake of a more cheerful ending.

Now when you read novels, study the gap between the climax and the end of the book, and see which writers manage to satisfy you with their dying chapters. It is not an easy thing to do well: everything is likely to seem like an anticlimax. The reader, however, does need to know the *effect* of the climax on the other characters, and will feel let down if this is not supplied.

There are, of course, exceptions to all of this: in some cases the climax will come at the very end of a story. This is so in Philippa Pearce's *A Dog So Small* where there is no need for further explanation after the true ending of the novel. This is a book which deserves close study as it is such a good example of developing your material from one small initial idea.

A Dog So Small

The story is simply about a boy's longing for a dog – the whole novel is about that. ('Be mean with your ideas', as we were told before.) In the first chapter, Ben thinks he is getting a dog for his birthday, but in fact he only gets a picture of a dog. The writer makes it difficult for herself by making Ben live within a large and supportive family, but even so he cannot have a dog because the family live in a flat in London. Even when his grandfather's dog Tilly unexpectedly has puppies, he cannot have a puppy because of where they live.

So obsessed, however, does he become with the idea of a dog, that the chihuahua in the picture his grandmother gave him for his birthday becomes his fantasy dog, following him everywhere, and being most

112

clearly visible to him when his eyes are shut. He neglects his school work, loses concentration and doesn't even care about Christmas, until finally this fantasy dog leads him into real danger . . .

You will remember, perhaps, that in the planning of this novel it was actually the ending that Philippa Pearce imagined very early on:

One of the scenes that came to me earliest of all was set on Hampstead Heath, late one summer evening. I know the Heath well, and that's when I like it best. Perhaps that was why I put my boy there then. For, when everyone else had gone home, he was still wandering on the Heath; he was the only thing you could see moving in the failing light. There was absolute stillness, too, until he called to somebody or something. I liked the dramatic way his voice cracked the silence. Then there was an answering sound from over the Heath – a dog barking, and out of the dusky distance a dog rushed towards him – a living dog for him alone. The boy and his dog met, overjoyed, and then they went over the Heath together, their shapes melting into the dusk again. And that, I realized, was the end of my story.

So, long before I had the beginning of the story, I had the end . . .

Eventually, because the daughters move away from home and the mother wants to be near them, the family shifts to a house near Hampstead Heath so that it does become possible for Ben to have a dog. So that all should now end happily? No, the writer still refuses to make it easy for her character or for herself. Ben has had nine months of hopeless longing for a dog and now finally he can have one of Tilly's puppies, but it has got bigger and is timid and isn't the sort of dog he wants at all. He still yearns after his perfect, his imaginary dog,

even giving the real dog its name, although it already
has a name of its own. He takes it to Hampstead
Heath and, in the gathering dusk, hopes that it will
go away.

He gave it a push: 'Go away then, you! Go!'
   The brown dog, nameless because no longer named,
moved away a little and then sat down. Ben tried to
shoo him, but he simply moved out of reach and sat
down again. Then Ben set off angrily over the Heath;
the brown dog got up and followed him at a little
distance . . .
   There was solitude, stillness of evening, dusk that
was turning the distant trees from green to black . . .
   Ben slowed his pace; he sat down on a slope com-
manding a wide expanse. He was alone on the Heath
now, except for the brown dog. The dog had sat
down in the middle distance and was gazing at Ben.
   Ben knew that, if he called the dog by the name he
was used to, he would surely come; but Ben did not
call him.

Then Ben realises when he can no longer see the
brown dog, that you can't have impossible things, and
that if 'you didn't have the possible things, then you had
nothing'. At the same time he remembers nice things
about the brown dog:

He remembered the warmth of the dog's body against
his own, as he had carried him; and the movement of
his body as he breathed; and the tickle of his curly
hair; and the way the dog had pressed up to him for
protection and had followed him even in hopeless-
ness.

The brown dog had gone farther off now, losing himself in dusk. Ben could not see him any longer. He stood up; he peered over the Heath. No . . .

Suddenly knowing what he had lost – whom he had lost, Ben shouted, 'Brown!'

He heard the dog's answering barks, even before he could see him. The dog was galloping towards him out of the dusk, but Ben went on calling: 'Brown-BrownBrownBrown!'

Brown dashed up to him, barking so shrilly that Ben had to crouch down and, with the dog's tongue slapping all over his face, put his arms round him and said steadyingly, 'It's all right, Brown! Quiet, quiet! I'm here!'

Then Ben stood up again, and Brown remained by his side, leaning against his leg, panting, loving him; and lovingly Ben said, 'It's late, Brown. Let's go home.'

It's well worth writing a novel just to fit an ending such as that.

What to me is so interesting about this novel is that it proceeds in such a single-minded way to its conclusion. Everything that is introduced into this novel has a bearing, either directly, or indirectly, on Ben's longing to have a dog, even down to the passages that his grandmother reads from the Bible; and hence the strength of its conclusion. Philippa Pearce also said of this novel that when you read it you think that the child can't have the dog because of his circumstances, but actually it was the other way round: *because* she imagined this child with the acute longing for a dog she then had to create such circumstances around him.

Stories are not usually presented, nor should they be,

in the chronological order of events. This may seem to be a strange thing to say, but won't be if you think about it. A story, in order to interest us, is in the business of holding back information. If you know someone who tells stories well, stories about what has happened to him or stories that he hears about, you will perhaps notice the way he rearranges his material for effect: the shaggy dog approach, for example, where the narrator deliberately delays getting to the point, and with the telling pause before the punch line. Stories may *appear* to be in chronological order, but if you look at them closely, you will see that this isn't so. A lot of rearrangement has to go on. Note too, that it is not the *material* that makes a story interesting, but rather *how* it is presented. In skilful hands practically anything can be turned into a good story.

You can't just hold back information, however. You have to let the reader know that something is, in fact, being held back, otherwise he or she can have no desire to find out about it. You have to tease the reader with half explanations, which we find all the time in the novels of Ruth Rendell/Barbara Vine. *Heartstones* is to be about poisoning, we know, but is this strange girl the poisoner, and if so, why is she uncertain that she is?

Presumably when we write a story we know the ending of it, at least by the time it gets published, and this perhaps is what we want to attract the reader towards but hide from him at the same time. I say 'at least by the time it gets published' because I think it is perfectly possible to write a novel without being entirely sure about where it is heading. Nevertheless, at the stage when we are rewriting it, we will need to put in little clues which will point towards the conclusion, so that the ending will seem to have arisen naturally.

When you read a story and are brought up short by something, it is likely to be one of these clues. You find yourself wondering: why has the writer bothered to describe the *toolshed* in so much detail? How boring! But *because* it sticks out, you will remember it and only later realise its importance.

If you tease out the actual story of a Barbara Vine mystery, like *A Dark-Adapted Eye*, you will be amazed at what you find. The story is quite simple and ordinary: ordinary in the sense of usual. It is just the sort of sensational item (apart from the hanging, of course) that you read about in the newspaper every day. A woman is to be hanged for the murder of her sister with a kitchen knife. The cause of contention? A boy of five who is the natural child of one of them, but brought up (perhaps) by the other.

But you don't know until well on in the book who has actually been murdered. And the sisters adore one another. And there is doubt, even at the end, about whose child Jamie actually was. All you know at the beginning is that Vera is to die at 8 am that morning: the rest is gradually revealed. For plotting skills, for learning how to keep your reader as near to the edge of (do I really have to say 'his or her' each time?) his chair as possible, you cannot do better than to study Barbara Vine.

TRY THIS!

- Discuss something that happened to you or that you observed which you found puzzling. What questions did it suggest to you? What sort of scenes and characters might arise from such an idea?

- List ten uncomfortable situations into which you could put a child of school age. Outline the climax to a novel based on one of these.

- Have a try at writing the climax to a novel based on a child's fear.

- Have a look at the pages between the climax and the ending in one of the novels you have been reading. Is this a satisfactory section? (You might consider, for example, whether its material is not only informative but delivered in an interesting way.)

- Write a few sentences about a book whose ending has stayed vividly in your mind since your childhood.

- Summarise the story of any novel in one paragraph and then say something about how the writer, in the working out of the plot, has rearranged his or her material for maximum effect.

CHAPTER 6

Novels and Short Stories (11+ Years) Further Aspects of Technique

CHARACTERISATION

Remember, first of all, as we said earlier, that you don't need to think of character in a vacuum: your character will be reacting in a finite number of situations. Give your main character a name – that will help for a start. Don't just choose any name: choose one that seems to fit your idea and your story. Once you select a name that you are happy with, bits of personality will start to attach themselves to it. I wanted an unusual name for the character in my novel, a name that perhaps no one had ever had before. So I chose one that could be seen to be derived from an Old Norse name. I called him Gunno, and then gave an ordinary name to the boy in the story who functions as a contrast to him. I called him Pete.

That at once gives you a start, and remember it is always useful to have contrasting characters. It underlines the qualities of your main character, and will help you in scenes in which both participate because their reactions will be different. At one point Pete kicks a dog: something that Gunno could never do, and something that haunts him, Gunno, and not Pete, afterwards.

Andrew and Victor are clearly contrasting characters in Jan Mark's *Thunder and Lightnings*. Andrew is from an educated, muddled, friendly household while Victor is from a sterile, cleanly and unaffectionate one. Yet Andrew is more ordinary than Victor, more predictable. At first you think it is Andrew, introduced in the opening chapter, who is to be the main character, but as soon as Victor, the boy who reads 'so slow [he] can't tell what's funny and what isn't' appears (in Chapter 4) he starts to take over the narrative.

He is introduced to us as being in disguise. Andrew thinks that Victor is a very fat boy with a very thin face. But when he gets closer:

Andrew realised that Victor was not fat at all. On the contrary, he was exceptionally thin; all of him, not just his head and legs. The fat part was made up of clothes. Andrew could see a white T-shirt, a red shirt, a blue sweater and a red sweater. Further down he wore a pair of black jeans with orange patches sewn over the knees and yellow patches on the hip pockets. Over it all he had an anorak so covered in badges and buttons that it was difficult to tell what colour it was.

At first Victor seems a quaint, even backward boy, not the sort of person Andrew is looking for as a friend. But then we start to wonder. At school, for example, he writes in such a way that the teacher is glad to avoid reading anything of his. Until finally, of course, we realise that Victor is extremely smart: that just as his

body and his writing are disguised so does he disguise
the nature of his mind from others. The story is set in
Norfolk and Victor's great passion is aeroplanes, in
particular the wonderful, heavy Lightnings that are soon
to be scrapped. Andrew asks why Victor keeps doing
projects on fish, when he doesn't even go fishing. Why
not do a project on aeroplanes?

*'I don't know,' said Victor. 'Yes, I do, though,' he
added, after thinking hard for a minute. 'If I started
doing that for school, I wouldn't be interested in them
any more. I don't care about fish, so I don't mind
doing them.'*

*'Why wouldn't you be interested in them at school?'
said Andrew. 'I thought the whole point of the
projects was to do something you liked.'*

*'Ah, yes,' said Victor. 'But it would be having to
like aeroplanes instead of just liking them. Every time
a Harrier went over I wouldn't be thinking, there go a
Harrier, I'd think, there goes my project. Then I
wouldn't want to look at it. School's like measles. That
spread.'*

You can see character being revealed here through
description and dialogue. Note the amused, often ironic
tone of the writing which appears to reveal Jan Mark's
attitude to the education system generally. 'Tone', as I
have mentioned before, reveals the attitude of a writer
to his (or her!) material and often to the audience as
well. It is a sort of slant or colouring given to a passage,
mainly through word choice.

Character can be revealed in quite small ways: the
woman who takes up two parking spaces to get the best
shade of a tree; the man who keeps switching his torch

on and off on the way out to the car; the teacher who
makes himself late for a meeting because a sparrow has
got caught in his room. Then there are the little phrases
that you will notice people repeating over and over
again. The person who, after every point he makes,
however fatuous, says: 'How does that sound?' as if in
need of constant support and affirmation. The person
who says 'Put it this way,' and then comes out with one
cliché or another. Examples are all around us and can be
used in our writing to help define character, especially,
perhaps, if we just want to do lightning sketches of some
of our adult characters. The main focus of children's
books for this age group tends to be on children, as we
know, although I always like books myself where some
sense of the adults, who after all do inhabit the
children's world, is given quite strongly.

Andrew's mother in *Thunder and Lightnings* is a warm,
muddly, whimsical character with very much the same
quality of humour in her conversation as Victor displays
in his. It is no wonder they get on so well. Here is a
passage which highlights some aspects of her
housekeeping, and provides an example of her
conversation. It is Victor (initially) who is speaking:

*'There's always coffee going at your house, isn't there?
Do your Mum keep that pot boiling all day?'*

*'It's not a pot, it's a percolator,' said Andrew. 'I
wish she'd buy instant coffee. She fills it up in the
morning and just keeps adding water all day. When it
comes out grey it's time for a new lot.'*

*'We have coffee at eleven in the morning and half
past three in the afternoon,' said Victor. 'Never in
between. I wouldn't care how grey that was if I could
just have that when I wanted it.'*

When they reached Andrew's house he left Victor
greeting the guinea-pigs and went in to light the gas
under the percolator. Mum was at the table, slapping
a foggy piece of pastry onto the top of a pie dish.

'Shepherd's pie,' she said. 'Plenty of vegetables, but
not very much shepherd. There was less meat on that
bone than I thought.'

'You don't make shepherd's pie with pastry,' said
Andrew.

'We're almost out of potatoes too,' said Mum.

You will notice also that the two households, Victor's
and Andrew's, are being contrasted.

If you think about it, when people are in groups, in
meetings or at dinner parties, for example, you are
sure to notice that some will dominate, some will
observe, and some will appear almost to fade away.
Children are people too; you get the same sense of
quite young children trying to dominate. You might
think about what characteristics make a leader; often
people will follow someone whom they don't
particularly like. This is another way of looking at
your characters: who is going to lead and who will
follow and why? (Joan Phipson's early novel, *The
Boundary Riders*, is very much about leadership, as
indeed is her later book *The Cats*.) The Australian
novelist, Elizabeth Jolley, says that she likes to get the
rhythm of a character through music: someone may
have a disco beat to them, she says. This will give
dimension to the character.

Remember too, that you get interesting mixes in
characters. You can have a mixture of bravado and
diffidence in the same person. Margaret Drabble's
(adult) novel, *The Millstone*, begins in this way:

*My career has always been marked by a strange mixture of
confidence and cowardice: almost, one might say, made by it.*

(The same might be said for Betsy Byars's character
Mouse, in *The Eighteenth Emergency*.) If you unite
opposing characteristics like this, you will have to work
harder to ensure that the character remains consistent.
Perhaps it is only in certain situations that one of these
attributes will be apparent.

There are many ways in which characters are
revealed in fiction as in life: you must look at how they
act, what they say and how they think. If there is a gap
between what people think and what they do then you
can exploit this for comic effect. How your character
feels about those around him is important too. You can
also use what other characters say about him, how they
react to him. If they admire him this can be a way of
building up your character.

But basically what needs to happen is for you to *care*
about your characters; once you do, everything else will
follow. You will start to think about them almost all the
time. For example, driving can become a dangerous
activity when you are longing for the lights to turn red,
or for somewhere to pull in, so that you can write down
a phrase that has come to you, or a line of dialogue that
clearly reveals a particular voice! You shouldn't ever
feel that you *are* that character; you should be aware of
him or her at some distance from yourself, so that you
are watching in a partly detached but kindly way. If you
steep yourself in your story and write a bit of it every
day, phrases will start to come to you all the
time – often first thing when you wake up in the
morning. And something that I should perhaps have said
earlier: if you think of a novel as having twenty

chapters, that will divide it up into manageable bites of 2500 words a chapter. If you write a chapter every week you'll be finished, at least on the first write through, in five months. Regular work on a novel will pay off in all sorts of ways, not only in that you will actually get the job done, but because your mind will be ticking over on it all the time and bringing you unexpected gifts even when you are not directly thinking about it.

SETTINGS

If you are having trouble with your plot or your characters, it can sometimes help to vary your setting a little more. This was a suggestion which Julie Watts made to me when I was writing *The House Guest*. Most of the scenes were set in an old house, with some at the beach. But when I put the characters in other places as well – in the park, in a graveyard, in a lonely area of scrub – somehow the novel managed to get moving again. This also seemed to bring out different aspects of the characters. I don't mean that you have to make big changes, like having the characters go for a holiday in a different town say, but just in the area where you have most of the action you may extend it a little: include a scene in a deli or up at the youth centre or in someone else's house. It is amazing how a fresh setting will add a bit of life to your story.

Writers get tired of the advice to write about what they know; but really it is true, and applies very much to location. If you set your story around the area where you live, it is so easy for you. You can go out and see what it is like: study how noisy it is at four o'clock in the afternoon, look at what people do on Sundays, take note of the street trees and how many houses are for sale. It is so easy to describe things that you know and can look at, so why don't you give yourself a head start? Sometimes when we are reading something we think, 'What a wonderful description! How detailed!' But think too that it is quite possible that the writer was studying the actual scene or object at the time.

Writers tend to think when they are starting off that their lives and neighbourhoods are very boring and should have nothing really to do with fiction. They feel they will have to write about Naples or Nice or Oxford or some place that seems glamorous to them. But it is quite clear when you are involved in a writing class that everybody's life is fascinating to other people, and this includes information about whatever neighbourhood they happen to be in. If you have any doubts about this think of the popularity of the British television series *Seven Up*, where audiences all over the world wait impatiently to see what has happened to their favourite (real life) characters after each seven-year gap.

Similarly it is always helpful to set your story in whatever season it is at the time of writing. In that way you can see what flowers are out, what trees are blossoming, and remind yourself of what it feels like to walk out into the extreme heat of an Australian summer, for example. Phyllis Whitney stresses how important it is to include sensory detail in your writing:

Wherever you go, collect sounds and odors, and the feel, even the taste, of things. And I don't mean only the taste of food. Dry, dusty air has a taste. So has fresh, salty sea air, or sunny country air, or air heavy with fog. In touching objects, think about how they feel. Are they warm or cold?

126

*Do they feel limp or hard, rough or smooth? What other
familiar objects do these things resemble? Don't rely only
on your fingers for touch sensation. How does snow feel
against your face? Or water against your body? How does
that inviting pillow feel behind your back?*

*If you make a habit of collecting details of this kind using
all of your senses, you will find your writing enriched and
enlivened far beyond the effort it will take. Children especially are lovers of detail, and they will prize your stories if
you can bring alive in words their everyday world, as well
as some new world to which your story introduces them.*

An excellent model for this is William Mayne. He is
often thought of as a difficult writer, yet one of the
charms of his writing is his ability to use homely
imagery to at once make accessible to children, to
everybody, what he describes:

*Whatever it was it had gone, and the morning was
still again, with the Minster bells still sounding up on
the hill like plates sinking and knocking together in a
big bowl of water.* (From his novel *It*)

Or here, from the same novel, in his description of the
sky:

*The strange sky was like grey velvet, soft-looking
cloud not far away, solid but streaked with light and
dark so that it looked a little untidy and in want of
steaming and ironing on the wrong side to become
smooth.*

His descriptions are always meticulous, as here:

There were fallen sycamore leaves, rolled like
gloves, among the beech leaves. Beech leaves are
waterproof in look, and hard-wearing, but the syca-
mores had begun to rub and wear and show their inner
threads. Alice crunched both sorts of leaf underfoot in
the settled slope of them at the bottom of the Eyell. (From *It*)

Or finally, in this passage taken from his recent novel
Gideon Ahoy!:

Outside, the green hillside was quiet itself, but noisy
with birds. Drops of resting rain fell from the leaves of
little trees and the growing ends of woodbine and ivy.
The sun shone down along the leaves and seemed to
make something hot, where a small mist rose.

No other writer, perhaps, would distinguish between
the hillside (quiet) and the hillside with birds (noisy).
Who else would think to call it 'resting' rain, or
distinguish, in such a context, the ends of the woodbine
and ivy as 'growing'?

But to return to you. Ask yourself what you know a
lot about: running a school camp, windsurfing, life-
saving, bushwalking, embroidery, gardening, cricket,
breeding dogs, singing, organising a family or whatever,
and then use that as background in your stories. Write
about what you know, and you will find, perhaps to
your surprise, that this will result in fresh and interesting
writing.

If you feel that you don't know much about anything,
then don't despair. Find out about something, not
necessarily something that you have a great interest in.
Find out about it and you will *become* interested in it.
Let's turn to Phyllis Whitney again, for she is such a

sensible writer. She came out of a bad slump once (a time when she felt that she had absolutely nothing to write about) on discovering this rule:

Interest follows action. *First, you do something – then you get interested. So many people think it should be the other way around and that you have to be interested before you care about doing anything. This, of course, gets you nowhere.*

She then describes how she pulled a subject out of the air, 'department store advertising,' and how this eventually led to her writing a story with, as its background, window displays in a department store.

DIALOGUE

Dialogue, as we've seen, is the most effective way of all of revealing character, but only the very best writers manage to distinguish their characters in the way in which they speak. Jane Austen, of course, manages it all the time. Anyone who has read her novels will know at once who the following speaker is:

'Mrs Bates, let me propose your venturing on one of these eggs. An egg boiled very soft is not unwholesome. Serle understands boiling an egg better than any body. I would not recommend an egg boiled by any body else – but you need not be afraid – they are very small, you see – one of our small eggs will not hurt you. Miss Bates, let Emma help you to a little bit of tart – a very little bit. Ours are all apple tarts. You need not be afraid of unwholesome preserves here. I do not advise the custard. Mrs Goddard,

*what say you to half a glass of wine? A small half glass – put into
a tumbler of water? I do not think it could disagree with you.'*

This is, of course, Mr Woodhouse in *Emma*. You can
see from the passage that Mr Woodhouse is elderly and
an invalid, his thoughts revolving very much round the
effect of food on the digestion. You will notice too that
he is courteous ('let me propose') and rather pompous
('I would not recommend') and while delightful in
fiction, might be rather a bore in real life. Note how his
ideas advance terribly slowly, in half steps. The boiling
of an egg takes up three sentences, and the apple tart
and custard four. The repetitions and qualifications in his
style help to reveal his extreme pernicketiness.

If you can do that, if you can make your characters
speak with distinctive voices, you can do everything.

When you start writing, it is often puzzling to know
what to put into direct speech and what to summarise in
a descriptive way. If we just keep reminding ourselves
that dialogue should always be a highlight, we won't go
far wrong. This extract from Jan Mark's title story
'Nothing to be Afraid Of' is spare, functional and
amusing as it stands, but would be much less effective if
rendered into direct speech:

*She saw Auntie Lynn to the front door and Anthea
heard them saying good-bye to each other. Mum almost
told Auntie Lynn to stop worrying and have a good
time, which would have been a mistake because Auntie
Lynn was going up North to a funeral.*

By the time a reader had waded through all the
'Goodbye Lynns' he or she would be falling quietly
asleep.

You probably wouldn't make the following mistake, but some people do when they are starting to write and it is very tiresome. They will say something in the narration and then repeat it in dialogue. For example:

The wombat emerged from its hole.
'The wombat is coming out of its hole, Mum!' he cried.

A very useful trick that you can pick up from Jan Mark's writing is the use of (for want of a better term) what I shall call 'half dialogue'. It's a way of moving out of narration and into dialogue very neatly without recording the whole conversation directly. Jan Mark often uses it for humorous effect and as a way of shifting from one group of characters to another. This extract is taken from her short story 'Charming!':

Alice Pitt might not have tuppence to bless herself with, but she had plenty between the ears.
'And plenty behind them,' said Gregory Beasley's mother.

Writers often take you straight into a scene of dialogue at the very beginning of their stories to get you off to a rapid start. This is how Louise Fitzhugh begins her novel *Harriet the Spy*:

Harriet was trying to explain to Sport how to play Town.
'See, first you make up the name of the town. Then you write down the names of all the people who live in it. You can't have too many or it gets too hard. I usually have twenty-five.'
'Ummmm.' Sport was tossing a football in the air. They

*were in the courtyard of Harriet's house on East Eighty-
seventh Street in Manhattan.*

    *'Then when you know who lives there, you make up
what they do. For instance, Mr Charles Hanley runs the
filling station on the corner.' Harriet spoke thoughtfully
as she squatted next to the big tree, bending so low
over her notebook that her long straight hair touched the
edges.*

    'Don'tcha wanta play football?' Sport asked.

The 'trying' to explain shows us that Sport is either
slow or uninterested in Harriet's game. Uninterested,
we decide, when we hear that he is tossing a football in
the air. Harriet, however, is absorbed in her imaginative
game. She speaks 'thoughtfully' we are told. The main
characters are at once clearly distinguished from one
another. A little description is also unfussily, unobtrusively
introduced within the lines of dialogue. We are told
where they are and where Harriet lives. We learn that
Harriet carries a notebook – so crucial to the whole plot
of the story – and that she has long, straight hair.

    Space Demons, by Gillian Rubinstein, opens in a similar
way, with the writer managing to insert information
about the characters during passages of dialogue:

*"Do you want to do anything else?" Ben asked. A
slight, fair-haired boy, he was smaller than Andrew
and a few weeks younger. He and Andrew had been
best friends in an unquestioning sort of way ever since
they had started kindergarten together. They were
now in the last year of primary school.*

    *"There's nothing to do!" Andrew said, turning
round from the window. The friendship was not an
entirely equal one. Ben Challis liked and admired*

*Andrew, but Andrew tended to consider Ben as a sort
of useful side-kick – he called all the shots and Ben
invariably went along with whatever he wanted. As a
result, Andrew did not always treat Ben very well.
This was one of those times.*

This device is intended as a way of 'sugaring the pill',
of providing information in the least painful of ways
without slowing up the story with a large block of
description.

You will notice from the examples given that
normally there will be a new line for a new speaker. It
is possible, however, to run on descriptive material after
the direct speech if it pertains in some way to what has
just been said. Publishers seem to have different styles on
this; if information is not very closely related, some
publishers will begin a new line for it, set off from the
dialogue. Publishers vary too in whether they like
double or single inverted commas. I would advise you to
use single ones as it means you don't need to be pressing
the shift key of your typewriter all the time. The
publisher can easily adjust this to his (or her) particular
house style at the editorial stage.

When you are writing dialogue try to make it sound
natural, not too formal. Go back over what you have
written. Try to break up what your characters are
saying into smaller segments. Make them repeat things
for emphasis. Tail off sometimes, when the meaning is
already clear. Try to vary your 'saids' a bit, not
necessarily by using different words like 'asked' and
'agreed' which can sound very contrived if you overdo
it, but by varying the structure of your sentences or by
adding an adverb to 'said': *he said anxiously*, for example.
Sometimes, of course, it will be clear who is speaking

and you won't need a 'he said' at all – but do check that it really *is* perfectly clear. The aim is to provide a certain amount of variety without being obtrusive and to ensure above all that the reader is never in any doubt about who is actually speaking. You will, as you keep writing, develop a 'feel' for it, although I know that it is irritating to be told something as vague as that when you are starting out. The short cut to developing this 'feel' is to study good models.

Phyllis Whitney has a really good tip on rearranging your sentence structure sometimes to obviate the need for a 'said' at all. She says:

Don't always use the common form:

"I'm awfully sorry about being late again, Mrs. Farmer,"
Mary Blake said, coming down from her high horse in a
split second.

Try it again this way:

Mary Blake came down from her high horse in a split
second. "I'm awfully sorry about being late again, Mrs.
Farmer."

Dialogue will sometimes key itself off as you write into unexpected jokes suggested by the words you have been using. Just follow it if you can. Again it is William Mayne who is a master of this. Perceptive adults and children enjoy the amount of punning that comes through in his dialogue.

'You're acting disagreeably,' said Mum.
'I'm not acting,' said Alice. 'I'm realling.' (From *It*)

Or in this exchange at the end of *No More School* about a child learning to read:

'They've learned quite a lot,' said Miss Oldroyd,
when she had talked to Bill and Susan. 'Bill can read
"Dog".'
  'It's the picture he reads,' said Shirley. 'Not the
word.'
  'It's a start,' said Miss Oldroyd.
  'It's a stop, too,' said Shirley.

A Swarm in May, an earlier (1955) title which first resulted in his books receiving critical attention, describes a really pleasant school which happens to be a cathedral school. You can see how nice it is by the teacher's comment to the boys after they have finished dinner: ' "Has everybody had too much?" said Mr. Ardent, trying to find takers for the last gooseberries.'

POINT OF VIEW

In a way I should probably have dealt with this first, because it is so important. If you are finding that it is very difficult to write in the way that you would like to, I think the quickest way of improving your writing is to keep to one point of view. If you can wander around inside every character's head, then there is no limit set on what material you can include in your story. It is hard, when we are inexperienced, to know what to put in.

  This one point of view may be either first person or third, but in either case you must restrict yourself to only (or mainly) what that one character can see, feel and experience. It means, for example, that you cannot include a scene where your point of view character is not present, unless he is eavesdropping somewhere nearby (a device often used by writers). Beginners often find it a quite frustrating and difficult technique: they find it hard to keep to the viewpoint, and aren't always aware when they have in fact moved out of it. The first-person form is much easier in this respect although (as touched upon in Chapter 4) it is more difficult in others. You then have to be so careful of your diction, of your word choice, throughout, as the thoughts all have to sound like those of an eight-year-old or thirteen-year-old or whatever. There is also a greater problem with it of making your character likeable. It is harder to find ways of building up the character without making it sound as if he (or she) is praising himself (or herself).

Sometimes it seems to be helpful to set the scene in an opening chapter *before* you move into the one viewpoint. As we found earlier (in the chapter on story books) this gives you the opportunity to describe your character without all the tedious looking into mirrors which is often resorted to. This is what I found myself doing in the opening chapter of *The House Guest*. The point of view does not shift to Gunno until page 5 which gave me a chance to describe him first, through the eyes of another character, Jess.

There is another character in the story that I became rather attached to. His name is Wally. At one stage when I was writing the book he kept taking whole chapters to himself. But I kept thinking about what my editor and my publisher's reader would say: 'shifting viewpoint' (the same fault as in my earlier stories). This meant, of course, that if I were going to write the novel from one viewpoint only, these chapters had to go. I found this very difficult to do, but I decided that it is true: you *do* cause a break in your story and reduce the emotional effect if you shift to another character in this way. You will have been aware of this yourself in stories, of the jerk you experience when suddenly you are pulled out of one character's mind, just as you were getting interested in it, and placed inside another's. In the end I managed to save bits of Wally by putting parts of his chapters into scenes of dialogue with Gunno.

I really enjoy reading books that are from one point of view: you do get an intensifying effect, a very strong emotional effect if the writer has made you identify with the character. Such a point of view can be very persuasive. In *Live Flesh* Ruth Rendell even makes us identify with a rapist and would-be murderer. As you read further into the book you find, to your horror, that you are almost hoping that he will get away with what he does. This is *not* the effect that we get from a book like Gary Crew's *Strange Objects* (winner of the 1991 Australian Children's Book of the Year Award for Older Readers). Although Steven Messenger is a similarly unpleasant character telling his story in the first person this time, this is only a part of a book based on 'documents'. Steven's present-day story is no more and no less important than the other 'documents' presented. Indeed the whole book is an illustration of alienation technique – where the reader is actively discouraged from becoming involved in the lives of the characters. This is a device familiar in the theatre and in adult fiction but unusual in children's writing.

It is rare to find a completely 'pure' third-person viewpoint. In Anita Brookner's *Hotel du Lac* (which you would swear was a 'pure' one-person viewpoint) you will find that on a few occasions the author slips into the minds of other characters like the hotel receptionist, or Edith Hope's publisher, in order to provide outside views of her. You have to balance it up: you gain and lose whatever you do. In the end you just have to decide if there is no other way of including material that seems crucial to you.

The single point of view is very useful for the creation of puzzles and mysteries, for, as in life, there is so much that the character isn't aware of; and it's satisfying too, because it's like life. He doesn't know what other people are thinking or feeling unless they tell him, for example, so the way is clear for plots based on misunderstandings and muddles.

All the mysteries and puzzles of Robert Cormier's *The Bumblebee Flies Anyway* depend on the fact that Barney, and the reader, do not realise that he too is terminally ill. The readers' ignorance is only possible because we are kept tightly inside Barney's viewpoint. Similarly, in Robert Westall's *The Scarecrows*, the intensity and suspense of the novel are generated by keeping us inside Simon's disturbed mind.

It is possible also to write with two (or even more) main character viewpoints. This is what Gillian Rubinstein does in *Space Demons* where Andrew and Elaine are given alternating chapters. You will notice, however, that the viewpoint does not shift within chapters, so that the reader soon becomes accustomed to the see-sawing of the text. This is the technique which is used often in films and in television scrials, where first one group of characters and then another is in focus. It is also a great help in creating suspense, because you can leave one character hanging over a cliff while you swing back to the other who is placidly darning socks. In a

novel the two stories will become more and more
entwined until the two protagonists come together at
the climax of the action. It may also be a way of
expanding your material, but I'm not really sure about
that.

Caroline Macdonald makes use of two, this time first-
person viewpoints, in *The Lake at the End of the World*.
There are no chapters in this novel and the writer
simply labels each alternating segment 'Hector' or
'Diana'. In her 1991 novel, *The Eye Witness*, segments are
numbered within chapters to indicate changing point of
view, this time involving several characters.

CHAPTER ENDINGS

Just as a very general guide, a story ending rounds
off – has a kind of dying fall to it, while a chapter
ending rounds the chapter off but at the same time
usually leads on in some way. There are no rules about
this, of course, and the following are just intended as
good examples from experienced writers.

Sometimes you will be told directly what is to be in
the next chapter as in this extract from Margaret
Mahy's *The Changeover*:

*It was a warm night, and she did not take her coat,
although she was not going to Sally's at all. She had lied
about her homework and lied about visiting Sally. She
was going several blocks through the dangerous night
to the very heart of the Gardendale subdivision and
was, of course, intending to talk to Sorry Carlisle,
seventh form prefect and secret witch.*

Or you can provide a pointer to how the next chapter will begin, like changing scenes in a film where you have to link them in some way. This is what Gillian Rubinstein does in one of the chapter endings in her gentle and beautifully developed story *Melanie and the Night Animal*:

By the time they had eaten the toasted sandwiches, come home again, put Mark to bed, and started work on the rest of the house, it was very late. Melanie went to bed in her new bedroom with packing cases all over the floor. She lay there listening to Mum and Dad and Mr Peters who had come in to help, running up and down stairs, throwing things across rooms, and stowing things away in cupboards, and then, suddenly, she was asleep.
Everyone forgot about the pizza outside the back door.

Colin Thiele sometimes anticipates future events in his chapter endings, as in this one describing the departure of a tuna boat in *Blue Fin*:

Out in the bay Dog Star *was dwindling into a shadow. It was the last anyone ever saw of her.*

You might think at first sight that this is a strange device but actually it produces a great deal of suspense. The reader is in advance of the characters and is watching, in a very tense way, to see what will happen when they know.

James Aldridge does something similar in this chapter ending from *The Broken Saddle*, although in much vaguer terms:

Nevertheless he knew that he and the pony were somehow at risk, though he didn't know what the risk was. And, as it turned out, the final effect of Mr Hunt's interest in the pony was not the one Eric was now afraid of. If anything the eventual result was quite unexpected, and, in its own way, much worse than his fear of Mr Hunt and his money.

Quite a lot of endings, however, simply function as a rounding off for the chapter itself. The following passage is taken from *Dicey's Song* by Cynthia Voigt. Dicey is feeling rather ambivalent about growing up, but, as conveyed in this simple image at the end of a chapter, is deciding that she will just have to accept it.

Dicey looked out over the tall marsh grasses, blowing in the wind. If the wind blew, the grasses had to bend with it. She wondered how they felt about that. "It's just," she said to her grandmother, "I have the feeling that I know who I am, only I'm not any more."

You really just have to work out what kind of chapter ending fits your story at any particular point.

The ending of a short story, on the other hand, must have a very final ring to it, as in Sophie Masson's short story with the marvellous title, 'It Only Happens Once'. (It is included in the Omnibus *After Dark* collection of stories.) The child in the story in effect has to choose between her parents, the distant father with the aura of glamour whom she longs to see again, or her mother who has worked so hard for years bringing up her children alone. She even takes them on holidays and has recently bought her daughter a longed-for telescope. She chooses her mother and her mother's possible future happiness:

Mum burst into tears. "You're a good girl," she sobbed. And I comforted her, thinking of the first adult step I'd have

to take in my life: write a letter to my father, explaining.
And yet Halley's comet was a once-in-a-lifetime experience.
Probably wouldn't be around when it happened again.

MAKING YOUR WRITING CONVINCING

I said something earlier about this (in Chapter 3) when I was talking about Peter Rabbit's jacket, but do keep it in mind. It's the small touches that convince. When Mary of *The Secret Garden* is staying at the English clergyman's house, one of the children wants to help her make a garden:

'Why don't you put a heap of stones there and pretend
it is a rockery?' he said. 'There in the middle,' and he
leaned over her to point.

Somehow it is that little qualifying touch, 'There in the middle,' that convinces you of the rest.

Or here is Erica on the bus to her aunt's in *Handles* by Jan Mark:

Taking a chance, she stood up and rang the bell once,
according to the instructions round the bell-push, which was
cream with a scarlet centre, like an uncooked jam tart.

The jam tart image convinces you that the journey really is taking place. Later, in the same novel, Erica teases Bunny, the man who works in Elsie's garage and is afraid of spiders because

'You can never tell which way they're going to run – all those
legs . . . With eight to choose from they could go anywhere.'

Erica shows him the spider in her cupped hands: 'The spider waved a leg suggestively through a crack between two fingers'. Just that one word 'suggestively' brings the whole scene to life.

And while we are on the subject of Jan Mark's spiders, how is this for an image of a spider in death?

Matthew thought it would have been nice to
find the Stone Age man as well, his bones folded neatly in
death like the spiders in the toolshed who folded their
legs into little wire baskets and died tidily.

This is taken from her second novel, *Under the Autumn Garden*.

Basically, of course, and underlying all this vivid selection of detail, is the writer's belief in her characters and her story. We too have to put our characters in real places that we know, on real days with particular weather conditions. We have to believe in them and care about them and at the same time describe accurately the small things that we see around us, like these fowls doing their homework in the dust:

Next door the fowls in the enclosure stalked about,
groaning happily, writing in the dust with a claw and
correcting with a sudden beak.

Now who do you think would have written that? Jan Mark or William Mayne?

FANTASY AND SCIENCE FICTION

Fantasy, as we noted in stories for younger children, can be a useful way of introducing an element of adventure into what we write. It may be far more than this, however. It can be a way of presenting our human experience more effectively and memorably than it may be possible to do in realistic fiction.

This is why there are, and have been, so many debates about the morality and worth of fantasy writing, with authors like Ursula Le Guin stating that fantasy is true and that is why people fear it, or J. R. R. Tolkien arguing in quite a different way that even if fantasy is escapist, what is the matter with that? In 'real life', he says, we applaud people for escaping from what is intolerable. Why should it be different in fiction?

Certainly fantasy, when it is done well, can be a way of enriching, of adding a new dimension to our experience. How else than through fantasy could Lucy Boston in her *Green Knowe* titles have shown the importance of history, of the present effect of past events and presences on the lives of each of us? How else could Philippa Pearce in *Tom's Midnight Garden* have shown a child that the personality remains, if not untouched, at least recognisable from childhood to old age, and that it is perfectly possible for a child to be the friend of somebody old? How better could Ursula Le Guin, in her poetic *Earthsea* trilogy, have shown that all our talents are of little use to us unless matched by a corresponding strength of character and control? And how better could Gillian Rubinstein in *Space Demons* and *Beyond the Labyrinth* have shown the dangers of lack of purpose and direction in contemporary Australian society?

Fantasy, at least for older readers, seems to fall within one of two main kinds. The writer may create a new world entirely – as in Tolkien's *Lord of the Rings* or Ursula Le Guin's *A Wizard of Earthsea* (and sequels). In fantasies like these the settings are imaginary and may be peopled by races and animals with no counterpart on earth. It is likely, however, that psychologically at least, the characters will not be foreign to us. Many modern stories, which postulate what our known world will be like 'at the end of the world', are really a variant of this kind of fantasy but are usually considered under the heading of 'science fiction' because they are futuristic. These, in a sense, all follow along behind George Orwell's *1984* where the intention is to point to what is worrying and dangerous in our present society. Titles that come to mind are Lee Harding's *Waiting for the End of the World*, John Christopher's *The Guardians*, Caroline Macdonald's *The Lake at the End of the World*, *Taronga* by Victor Kelleher and Isobelle Carmody's *Obernewtyn* chronicles.

Alternatively, some strange element may be introduced into the existing world and made to seem possible within it. This strange element very often has to do with time. In *Tom's Midnight Garden* Tom is able to move backwards in time, whereas Jack, in Caroline Macdonald's *The Eye Witness*, moves forwards. It may also have to do with 'haunting' of some kind, as in Margaret Mahy's *The Haunting* and *The Changeover* or in Penelope Lively's *The Ghost of Thomas Kempe*. Or it could be that a person from another planet is introduced (as in Patricia Wrightson's *Down to Earth* or Gillian Rubinstein's *Beyond the Labyrinth*), the purpose here often being to highlight how very strange some of our 'ordinary' activities and ways of looking at things actually are, if we are able to view them impartially from the outside. Where an alien is introduced, as here, the book tends to be considered (like fiction about future worlds and having the same sort of purpose) under the heading of 'science fiction' rather than fantasy. But more of this later.

In a fantasy of this second kind, where an 'impossible' element is introduced into what would otherwise be realistic fiction, it must be prepared for very carefully indeed. The fantasy element will be outside the rules of our known world, but we must make it appear *convincing* for all that. Philippa Pearce prepares us carefully for the transition in time with information about the old clock, for example, and by providing the reason why Tom is often awake at midnight. For readers older than this, stories often work well where the fantasy element is linked to some psychological problem that the protagonist is experiencing. You can then interpret what happens to him or her either as fantasy or as being a result of this psychological disturbance. In *Space Demons* Andrew is able physically to enter a computer and take part in an actual game within it. But this is prepared for by Andrew being so confused and upset by his parents' impending break-up that he becomes totally absorbed in his computer game. Similarly in Lee Harding's *Displaced Person* we wonder if Graham really becomes invisible in the real world or if he only believes that he does. Is he suffering from some kind of psychological disturbance or has he really been 'displaced'? This kind of ambiguity is often crucial to the credibility of a story or at least to its acceptance by different kinds of readers.

Where you have your character disappear into another world, one that is in some way within the real world or existing in parallel to it, how you write up

your protagonist's actual moments of entering and
leaving this other world is crucial to the success of your
story. (Do look at how Ruth Park handles this in her
fine novel *Playing Beatie Bow*.) You can't simply move in
one sentence from a world where normal restrictions
apply to a situation where anything is possible. Although
our experiences in dreams make us more receptive,
perhaps, to fantasy worlds, it is always very
disappointing to find at the end of a story that it was
'only a dream'. The fantasy element has to be given the
credence that we would give to any other aspect of the
novel. Nevertheless some step has been taken which is
not possible in the world as we know it. As writers we
just want to make it *appear* to be possible at a certain
time and under certain conditions.

Fantasy, then, is clearly not an easy option for the
writer – or for the reader, for that matter. Because of
the leap in credibility that the fantasy writer demands
from his or her material, setting and characterisation
have to be very strongly realised – for these will help to
evoke belief in what is really unbelievable. Tolkien
makes us believe in the landscape of *The Hobbit*; we
respond at once to the prickly and completely
recognisable character of Ged in *A Wizard of Earthsea*.
Writers also have to make their stories appear logical as
far as it is possible to do this by having events follow, as
in realistic fiction, from the personalities of their
characters. In *Space Demons* everything follows logically
from the personalities of the players involved. Similarly,
in *The Lake at the End of the World*, Caroline Macdonald
has worked out extremely carefully how the two groups
of people came to survive at all and what difficulties
they had to overcome.

I suspect too that the writer must also be convinced of

the *value* of what he or she is doing: must believe that there is no other way in which the story could be told as effectively. For example, the best book both in a literary and in a *healing* sense that I have read about parental separation and its impact on the child is Ruth Park's *Playing Beatie Bow*. Abigail can't understand how her father could have left her mother and herself (especially herself) for 'Miss Thingo', as she bitterly refers to her. She has let the idea of it corrode her life. Through a time-slip device she finds herself, at the age of fourteen, in nineteenth century Sydney and in the position of 'Miss Thingo' in somebody else's life.

So far I have indicated that children's novels are considered to be science fiction rather than fantasy where they are set in the future or where a character from another planet is introduced. Any story where some scientifically-based idea is fundamental to the plot (like a dying planet, a biological experiment or a space journey) would of course also be categorised in this way.

But is this really helpful? Both science fiction and fantasy are non-realistic forms of fiction, and both share the same key element: there is something in the story which we know to be scientifically impossible. But in science fiction the explanation for this is scientific or pseudo-scientific; in fantasy it is magical. And both require the reader to suspend disbelief: either by accepting magic (the fantasy form) or by being prepared to accept some extension of the laws of science in a plausible way.

The matter may seem to be complicated by the fact that many writers cut across these categories. Although we may wish to classify Caroline Macdonald's *The Lake at the End of the World* as science fiction, it does contain an element that is pure fantasy: the special power of the lake. Similarly *The Eye Witness*, again about a future world, could be considered as science fiction, but it contains an important fantasy element in its treatment of time. Conversely, Isobelle Carmody's *The Farseekers*, although futuristic, has far more in common with other quest fantasies than with books we might label as science fiction.

Science fiction, at least in adult writing, used to presuppose some grasp of current knowledge in a particular field, perhaps relating to biology or physics or astronomy. Aldous Huxley's *Brave New World* is an early and influential example. The writer, as you will remember, envisages a world of human engineering, with the race being raised in laboratories so that instead of individuals we have Alpha, Beta, Gamma, etc., types designed specifically to fill jobs in the society appropriate to their (given) intelligence levels.

Science fiction, in this stricter sense, is rare in children's writing. Some books which may appear to be science fiction are really basically fantasy in science fiction guise, like Robin Klein's *Halfway Across the Galaxy and Turn Left*. The 'end of the world' novels may appear to have some connection with science and hence with science fiction but really the world which they create is often basically our own world in a slightly exaggerated form.

The categories are also unclear in adult writing, and a collection of Australian 'speculative' stories published in 1992, *Glass Reptile Breakout*, was described by one critic (Katherine Cummings in the *Sydney Morning Herald*) as 'an eclectic collection, placing 'hard' science fiction . . . alongside fantasy . . . and science-fantasy.' Indeed many writers now, both for children and for adults, seem to be

happier with the more general and vaguer label
'speculative' to describe their fiction. It may well be that
the attempt to classify books according to their content
is bound to fail. As we found when we looked at the
question of originality, it always makes more sense to
talk about *approach* rather than content. It would be
possible, for example, to handle a time-slip element in a
scientific way rather than in the more usual fantasy
mode.

You can see then that the line currently drawn
between science fiction and fantasy is a rather wavering
and shifting one. I don't think this matters as far as our
own writing is concerned; we must just write our stories
in the way that we want to and as best we can and let
other people attempt to classify them (if they wish!).

All the reading and advice in the world won't help us
unless we are actually prepared to write. What we need
to do is to attach a board above our desks with Dr
Johnson's wise words upon it:

A man may write at any time if he will set himself doggedly to it.

And 'doggedly' is the right word, very often.

All the planning in the world won't help either unless
we actually sit down and write. And really, when I
think back, the only stories of mine that had any sort of
plan were those whose end was somehow built into the
beginning, like *Heffalump?*, *Parrot Fashion* and, I suppose,
The 89th Kitten. With the rest I just sat down with a bit
of an idea or even an opening sentence or perhaps a title
that I liked, and hoped for the best. *Pomily's Wish*, I
remember, developed in a strange way. I wrote one
paragraph and polished it until I thought it sounded
right, and then I wrote the next one, and did the same,

and so on. I had no idea where the story was heading. People do say, though, that there are in fact only three kinds of story: stories that are based on a quest, a rescue or a desire for revenge. That seems incredible, but it is not easy to think of exceptions to it. So perhaps if we get stuck in our plotting, we can always remind ourselves of that. J. R. R. Tolkien, one-time Professor of Anglo-Saxon at Oxford, was sitting in his study one day when the following sentence came into his head: 'In a hole in the ground there lived a hobbit'. He had no idea what it meant.

In the end we all have to face the terror of the blank page. Just write down something, anything, and the blankness and the terror will go away.

TRY THIS!

- Write about a fictional character of your own that you feel interested in. What is his or her name and why? What are his or her main characteristics? Into what sort of situations are these characteristics likely to lead the character? How does your character speak, phrase things? Treat us to a few lines of dialogue.

- What is your own personal setting? Describe your house and neighbourhood in such a way that you make clear what your feelings are in relation to both. (Don't forget the other people who live there!)

- If you were writing a novel, and wanted to put this very day in it, what aspects of the season, weather, plants and so on would you include?

- Have a try at writing the opening of a novel in dialogue, where the dialogue reveals character.

- Write a scene from a novel first of all in the first person and then in the third, but restricting yourself in each case to what one character can see, feel and experience.

- Study scene changes in any contemporary film. What techniques are used to link the scenes together?

CHAPTER 7

Editing Your Own Work

GETTING STARTED

I always think this is the really nice part. You've got your story down even if in an admittedly rough form, but still it is there and you can relax about it. Now, at your leisure, all you have to do is polish.

First of all we have to cultivate an air of detachment. Try to pretend that this is someone else's story and look at it as dispassionately as you can. Sheridan's words help: 'Easy writing's vile hard reading'. And the reverse is also true. Some writers believe that it also helps, in acquiring this air of detachment, to put your work aside for a few weeks *before* revising it. The danger is, of course, that you won't get back to it! You just have to work out what is the best method for you. Remember too that you are going to have to cultivate this air of detachment later on when your editor has suggestions for you.

You must, however, check that your story is in fact at the polishing stage. Ask yourself questions like the following:

Is there too much summarising in the story? Should I have given scenes directly that I have merely summarised or even left out altogether?

Have I skipped the climax or is it developed as the high point and indeed the turning point of the story?

Would my reader feel involved with the characters? Would he (or she) care about the fate of the main character? Do I care?

Is the ending a satisfying one? Does it leave any questions unanswered that should have been answered?

Is the structure of my story as tight as I can get it?

Is my story likely to give the reader an emotional experience?

If you are happy with your answers to the above questions, especially to the one about structure, now is the time to start polishing your work. You daren't polish before this as you will become so much attached to your words and expressions that you will find it almost impossible to change anything.

Be sure to reward yourself as you go along. Don't just look for faults: give yourself ticks and double ticks for parts that are nicely done. Then your task is to bring up the surrounding sections to the same level.

There are certain standard things to look for, which could come under headings like the following:

lack of clarity
ambiguity
clumsiness of wording
tailing off of sentences and paragraphs
unnecessary repetitions
weak punctuation
halting or 'lumpy' prose (that is, writing which is
lacking in rhythm, or which holds you up as you read it,
possibly because parts of your sentence are in the wrong
place)
flatness of effect (which may result from a lack of
emotional effect which is linked with pacing).

Let's look first at:

Repetition
You will be surprised at just how many unnecessary
repetitions will have crept into your text. Sometimes it
is almost as if we have adopted a favourite word, like a
modifier such as 'maybe' or 'perhaps' or 'however' or
'somehow', and somehow(!) it keeps appearing in the
text for two or three pages. You can almost tell how
many pages you did in one go, for the word will appear
in those pages and then suddenly disappear. The surest
way of checking for these is to read your work
aloud – the eye alone is likely to miss some of them.
    Sometimes it can be quite a trouble to find another
word that will do equally as well, but we may be
having difficulty because we are trying to change the
wrong instance of the word. Consider the following
sentences:

*The dog looked up at him out of tragic brown eyes, liquidy
looking and almond in shape.*

The 'looked' followed by 'looking' is clumsy. It is perfectly possible to substitute 'stared' for 'looked'.

Gunno thought of what he had read with a growing excitement, and his thoughts swung back and encompassed Hugh in them.

Here you might consider substituting 'reflected on' for 'thought of'.

But finally the truck that came to destroy the milk stand came in the night.

Here we could substitute 'the truck that was used'.

Never confuse a clumsy repetition with an intentional one. Sometimes you will want to repeat a word or a phrase for effect, and your editor may not realise this and will mark it out. Always fight for your original in this case: not all repetitions are clumsy ones. Think of Hans Christian Andersen, for example, full of repetitions but none of them clumsy, as in this extract from 'The Ugly Duckling':

The winter grew colder and colder; he was obliged to swim about on the water to keep it from freezing, but every night the space on which he swam became smaller and smaller.

Clumsy sounds

Watch out too for clumsy sounds. Again this is picked up by reading your work aloud.

He started stopping for their lone milk churn.

'Started stopping' sounds clumsy, not only in the

sound but perhaps because the meaning carries an apparent contradiction. Substitute 'began to stop'.

Sentences and paragraphs that tail off

Always end sentences on a strong note. For example, you may decide to change 'He didn't lose interest in the book though', where 'though' weakens the whole sentence, to the more definite, 'But he didn't lose interest in the book'.

Similarly, always put the strongest sentence in a paragraph at the end.

'Look,' said Pete again, still trying to be conciliatory. 'Stow it, Gunno. We couldn't manage without you, you know that. These great plans you draw, the way you remember everything.'

In this example the sentence beginning 'We couldn't manage . . .' needs to be shifted to the end as it is stronger than the present last sentence which is simply an illustration of this point. It is better to say:

'Look,' said Pete again, still trying to be conciliatory. 'Stow it, Gunno. These great plans you draw, the way you remember everything. We couldn't manage without you, you know that.'

Reorganising your sentence

Sometimes the words in your sentence just need shifting around to get maximum effect from them. This is one of the most interesting parts of revision because it makes you work out precisely what you want to say. With words in the wrong position your meaning can be unclear or ambiguous, or simply not sufficiently pointed, and your sentence can sound chopped up or clumsy in some other way.

All houses that were empty of their owners seemed hushed, but this one to Gunno seemed especially quiet.

'To Gunno' is in the wrong position, giving the sentence a chopped up effect and interrupting the flow of 'this one seemed especially quiet.' Change it to read:

All houses that were empty of their owners seemed hushed, but to Gunno this one seemed especially quiet.

Hugh turned the torch beam on Gunno's face again and then away.

You can strengthen the effect of this sentence by altering the position of 'again'. The word gains force if put next to 'torch beam'.

Hugh turned the torch beam again on Gunno's face and then away.

Anne opened the door and turned back to look at him. He felt now she was really looking at him, not tracing resemblances to her son.

You can strengthen the idea here by shifting the word 'really'. You want the emphasis to fall not on 'really looking' but on 'really at him'.

He felt now she was looking really at him, not tracing resemblances to her son.

Just write something down, anything.

You can improve this by putting the 'something' and

'anything' together. This allows for a building-up effect, with a natural stress now falling on 'anything':

Just write down something, anything.

What we need to do is to attach a board with Dr Johnson's wise words on it above our desks.

This can be improved by shifting the position of 'above our desks'. The phrase properly belongs with 'board'. Having it in the above position not only results in a chopped up effect but ends the sentence on a weak note.

What we need to do is to attach a board above our desks with Dr Johnson's wise words upon it.

I have also changed 'on' to 'upon' which seems stronger and more pointed, more definite.

Checking your pronouns

As a general rule use 'he' or 'she' for your character (once you have established what their name is) unless it is unclear to whom you are referring. It is very tedious to find someone's name used constantly in a piece of prose. You will have to use the character's proper name at the beginning of each new chapter, of course. You will also wish to use it too whenever you want the emotive effect, either softening or hardening, which is often supplied by simply naming the character. Sometimes you may wish to use the pronoun to create an air of mystery. This is sometimes done at the very beginning of a novel so that the reader will ask, 'Who is this? What is he doing? Why am I supposed to be interested in this?'

Look for neater and more accurate ways
To his left the pylon rose rigid to the sky, the light dancing on the wires that he could see plunging down one slope and up the next to a further pylon.

'That he could see plunging' is distracting because it changes the focus from the scene to the viewer. It is better to take Gunno out of it and say simply:

To his left the pylon rose rigid to the sky, the light dancing on the wires that plunged down one slope and up the next to a further pylon.

In *The Black Duck*, Tom is annoyed by the present he has been given for his birthday, and he walks out of the room. The first version came out like this:

Tom, his face hot, marched out, kicking the wheel of his new trike as he went.

But I don't think it is clear that he is wheeling his bike at the same time, nor is it clear how annoyed he is. I changed it to:

Tom, his face hot, marched out, taking his trike with him but kicking its wheel viciously as he went.

Leave out the obvious
Only, now that the birds had fallen silent a strange waiting feeling seemed to have fallen on the bush, swimming uneasily in the heat. He shivered although it was now so hot.

'Swimming uneasily in the heat' is a distraction: if you give too much detail you weaken the effect. The important thing here about the bush is the 'waiting feeling', not the heat shimmer:

Only, now that the birds had fallen silent a strange waiting feeling seemed to have fallen on the bush. He shivered although it was now so hot.

(Gunno is seizing the rope from Hugh.) *'Impatient, aren't you?' muttered Hugh, obviously surprised at what seemed to be Gunno's rudeness, but he let him take it.*

Hugh is clearly taken aback. There is no need to state the obvious. All that is required is:

'Impatient, aren't you?' muttered Hugh, but he let him take it.

Note also that we had to change the viewpoint to Hugh in order to put the unnecessary insertion in.

These unwanted bits often crop up in relation to characters' feelings. Be careful not to overstate these, particularly at an important place in the narrative, as here, at the end of a chapter:

He looked down at the dog, feeling trapped, feeling desperate, waiting for her ears to go back, waiting for the first sign that Geoffrey had come home. He had never felt more miserable in his life.

The last sentence is banal and obvious: Gunno's feelings are already perfectly clear without it.

But, although he always checked, there had never been a letter, never a card even, from Hugh. It was as if he had been wiped off the face of the earth.

Leave out the last awful sentence. It's interesting how often we find that we are writing in clichés when we try to put in these grand summational sentences.

Alter in the direction of being more specific

He looked around him at the black-trunked wattles and thought of Wally, of the graveyard. In August the wattle there would hang rich over the fence, cascading alongside Wally's favourite grave.

But I want to show that he feels *reassured*, thinking of Wally, and this doesn't come through. So let's alter it to:

He looked around him, thankfully, at the sanity of the black-trunked wattles and thought of Wally, of the graveyard.

That conveys his feeling, the need to hang on to what he knows. But the second sentence too needs attention. Let's change it to:

There in August the wattle hung rich over the fence, cascading down beside Wally's favourite grave.

Opening the sentence with 'There' immediately strengthens it and forms a link with the preceding sentence. 'Hung' is stronger than 'would hang' because it suggests the certainty of repeated and predictable action, and 'down beside' is more specific, more accurate than the vaguer 'alongside'.

But Gunno was looking upwards, listening. It was the same small noise he could hear – a whistling noise – but now it was growing.

'Small' and 'whistling' are too general for what I want here. The words suggest that I haven't properly imagined this section. Let's try again, in the direction of being more specific.

But Gunno was looking upwards, listening. It was the same strange, frail noise he could hear – a faint, small, singing sound – but now it was growing.

Even small touches can make a difference:

The passage was narrowing again, change to, *The passage was narrowing still more.*

Sometimes you just need an adjective. Change, *The walls of the room and the arch overhead were stretching . . .* to, *The walls of the stone room and the arch overhead were stretching . . .*

You may just need to change a participle to the stronger mood of the verb, as here:

He gazed in despair at the piles of shadowy grey rocks lying everywhere across the earth floor.

To change 'lying' to the more definite 'that lay' strengthens the sentence:

He gazed in despair at the piles of shadowy grey rocks that lay everywhere across the earth floor.

By the way, if you are interested in the moods of verbs(!) and in learning more about grammar, style and punctuation, a most useful guide is *The Elements of Style* by William Strunk, Jr. and our own E. B. White (author of *Charlotte's Web*). It is an old book now (first published in 1959) but its advice is still invaluable. It is in print and is published by Macmillan.

Pacing: slowing up for effect

Often you will need to slow up what you are saying in order to create the effect that you want. It may be a character's reaction which you are describing:

'I feel as if I've made you up,' said Hugh, shaking his head. 'Oh well, let's have a look at this lunch of yours.'

That's not nearly enough to show Hugh's amazement at Gunno's very existence. Let's slow up his reaction:

'I feel as if I've made you up,' said Hugh, shaking his head. 'It's odd, I was just thinking about you today – at least about your name . . . ' His voice trailed off. Then, after a pause while he kept staring at Gunno, 'Oh well, let's have a look at this lunch of yours.'

The naming of the dog is crucial to the plot in *The House Guest*, so that when Anne asks Gunno what he has called the dog I wanted to delay the information as much as possible. I did this by recording his thoughts and feelings as well as his actual words:

'Tell me, Gunnar, what did you call the dog? Our dog, I mean.'
    Rob, Gunno thought. Hugh had called it Rob. Thought it was a male pup. A hairy dog, not smooth. 'Well, Pooch mainly. Hound, things like that.'
    'You didn't give her a name?'
    Again the feeling of desolation. It had been Hugh's dog after all. A jolly dog. 'Yes,' he said slowly, 'I did. I think of dogs being male and cats being female . . . '

Anne was nodding as if she understood.
'So I called her . . . '
'Yes?'
'I called her Sam.'

Notice how you can delay giving the information just by breaking off what your character is saying.

Often you can slow up for a particular effect by the use of a simple repetition. Consider the following sentence:

He looked up – but where two trees had stood there were now three very tall trees with reddish straggly bark, not two as he had remembered.

This does not give proper attention to what you want to appear significant and strange to the reader. Try altering it in this way:

He looked up – but where two trees had stood there were now three: three very tall trees with reddish straggly bark, not two as he had remembered.

Just the insertion of the word 'three' puts the emphasis where you want it by providing a pause which neatens and gives point to the whole sentence. This, by the way, has the ring of a chapter ending: it rounds off but leads on at the same time, and has a kind of (minor) dying fall.

If you want to emphasise something you have to build up to it – by *delaying* the revelation of whatever it is. In a sense you are providing a frame for it as if you were setting off a picture. Consider this example from *The Black Duck*:

There was something Tom had been trying not to think all the time he had been sitting with Squeak Toy. But now it kept coming into his head. It was to do with the dam. Squeak Toy wouldn't have her big dam any more to swim in.

Or this one from *Pomily's Wish*. Great Uncle Bernard tells the young mice frightening stories. What follows is the build-up to the first story:

Great Uncle Bernard always took a long time to get settled. He would smooth back his whiskers and arrange his tail, examine his paws and brush the crumbs from his coat. But at last he would begin, and this is the very first story that he told them.

Originally for the last sentence I had: 'This is the first story that he told them.' You can see how bald that sounds compared with what we have now: a sentence which provides a link with the preceding one and delays the delivery of the first story.

Too many adjectives?

Sometimes you can spoil the effect of a description by having it too weighted down with adjectives which compete with one another for attention. Often you can get the same effect by converting one of the adjectives into another part of speech. In the following example 'glistening' competes rather with 'white':

He was still clutching the torch and as he swarmed up the rope the beam fell on the walls picking out white glistening flecks.

You can alter this quite simply by using a verb so that both adjectival ideas are given equal weight:

He was still clutching the torch and as he swarmed up the rope the beam fell on the walls picking out white flecks that glistened.

Adjective in the wrong place?
Sometimes you feel the need for a word within a sentence, but actually you have it qualifying the wrong noun. Take this example:

He felt a thick wave of darkness pass over him.

Can waves be 'thick'? Is that really what you mean? Maybe it is the other noun that you want to qualify:

He felt a wave of thick darkness pass over him.

That makes much more sense, and still preserves the balance which the adjective gives to the sentence.

GENERAL POLISHING

Let's look now at some sentences which have been polished in various ways to see if we can come to any general conclusions about the process involved.

He walked over to it [the waterhole] *and looked at the straight red sides of it, the muddy water still managing to reflect the tangle of bush around.*

I suppose that is all right in its way, although the 'of it' is ugly after the 'to it'. It doesn't seem to have terribly much point, however, as description. Perhaps if you shift the emphasis from the viewed to the viewer, you can get the description to say something about your character and at the same time suggest a significance for the dam which will become clear later on:

He walked over to it and stared in. It was dark and muddy but drew your eyes the way water always did.

Compare the following two versions:

He felt again, but in a subdued way this time, the rush of the air, the tumble of the earth, the dirt in his mouth. He winced, and as the earth settled, the calm of the bush returned. He thought of the blue hills of the distance, the stringy barks in threes as in the photo, the brown water of the tiny dam.

Gunno felt once more, but in a subdued way this time, the rush of the air, the tumble of the earth, the dirt in his mouth. He winced, and as the earth settled, he saw again the water world of leaves and swaying branches, the hills that smoked with distance, the pylons stretching, the brown of the waterhole that he had seen, restored, from the stretcher.

The first sentence is much the same except that I have substituted 'once more' for 'again' as I wanted to use 'again' in the next sentence. The next two sentences, however, have been turned into one. The general statement, 'the calm of the bush returned', has been omitted and the more specific elements of the former scene put there instead, finishing with the crucial one about the dam. I was trying to make the scene clear with these descriptive phrases, but even more I was attempting to give the passage a kind of hypnotic effect to echo the sense of peace Hugh's place had initially given to him.

Here is an earlier and a later version of a passage

describing Gunno riding his bike down the steep road from Upper Sturt to Hawthorndene:

The coming back was quick but worrying, it was so steep. Gunno alternated between exhilaration and moments of pure terror as his bike whizzed down the slopes at speeds it had never dreamt of before.

He rode back with the wind, fast and bending almost recklessly into the curves. He caught glimpses of the sea. He tried to think of Hugh again, of the scrub . . . He raced down the last steep slope. His face burned in the wind.

I like the second version better, perhaps because it is a little indirect. You get a sense of his speed and of his mood without it being spelt out too much. You are not told how he feels: you are left to infer it.

Here again is an earlier and a last version of the same idea:

He wobbled past the cemetery, carefully not looking in – he didn't want to see the blank grave where Wally wouldn't be – and pushed his way towards Blackwood against the wind to the turn-off in to Hawthorndene.

He wobbled past the cemetery, carefully not looking in at the blank grave where Wally wouldn't be, and pushed his way against the wind to the turn-off into Hawthorndene.

You don't really need to hold up your sentence to say 'he didn't want to see'. The second version is neater, more concise. Similarly we don't need to clog up the sentence with the unnecessary detail about Blackwood.

At one point in *The House Guest*, when Gunno is

chasing Hugh down the tunnel, I wanted to convey his feeling of extreme nervousness and tension. It seemed to me to have to do with a naked feeling that one gets around the heart in situations of extreme stress. I had a lot of trouble with the expression of this. Here are some of the earlier versions:

His heart felt fragile, as if it were beating in the air.

That's the sort of idea, but 'beating in the air' isn't really clear. Let's try 'exposed' instead:

His heart felt fragile, as if it were exposed to the air.

That's clearer, but a bit bald. I finally settled for this version:

The sick taste was back in his mouth and his heart felt shrunken and fragile as if it were exposed to air.

When you are working on a story or a novel you will soon find that it is writing itself in a particular style. And really many of the alterations which you will make to your wording will be in the direction of enforcing this particular style, of making the style consistent throughout.

PUNCTUATION

Children need the best punctuation that's going. The purpose of punctuation is to clarify meaning, in a sense to compensate for what is supplied through techniques like pauses and emphasis in the spoken word.

Our aim should be to make use of all forms of punctuation. It is interesting to find that many people commonly only use the comma and full stop in their writing, perhaps thinking (wrongly) that anything further than this is too sophisticated for children. This idea did not trouble writers like Beatrix Potter and Rudyard Kipling and shouldn't trouble us.

It is helpful to consider the functions of various forms of punctuation. Let's start with the bracket.

The bracket

If you put something in a bracket within a sentence it is almost in the nature of an aside. If it were to be left out, the sentence would still make complete sense, as in the following examples:

'Well, boy,' he said to her, (all dogs were males to him) looking around for something to bring her within the circle of well being too.

That was what he did on the Sunday after he had 'visited' (as he phrased it in his mind) the big house for the second time.

By the way, you don't need a comma after the bracket in this kind of self-contained structure.

(Brackets, of course, in much the same way, may contain whole sentences.) The bracket is a pleasant and helpful device, used, for example, to convey humour, information or authorial comment but it mustn't be over-used. If it is, its effectiveness will dwindle until it becomes a mannerism.

A bracket can also be useful for tidying up a sentence that is getting too long or complicated, as in the following example:

When you watch a soapie, notice how close the protagonist comes to achieving his goal, like winning the love of the beautiful girl, perhaps, time after time, but some obstacle always appears at the last minute.

If we use a bracket here, shift the position of 'time after time' and leave out the 'perhaps', the sentence will be easier to read and the meaning clearer:

When you watch a soapie, notice how close the protagonist comes to achieving his goal time after time (like winning the love of the beautiful girl), but some obstacle always appears at the last minute.

The comma
The only point I want to make here is that sometimes you need a comma to stop the eye from linking two words together. It will not be a usual place for a comma, but this is the reason for putting it in – to halt a false connection. If you read the section aloud and stumble, you need a comma. Consider this sentence:

What follows is chapter nine of The Black Duck, *and it is a chapter my editor asked me to add to show how Tom felt during the night that he was lost.*

You may stumble when you read this, as the 'to' which goes with 'show' seems to be connecting with 'to add' – 'to add to'. If you put in a comma after 'add', you prevent this. The sentence now reads:

What follows is chapter nine of The Black Duck, *and it is a chapter my editor asked me to add, to show how Tom felt during the night that he was lost.*

The single dash

The single dash can be useful to set off something in your sentence, thereby drawing attention to it:

But he had expected some sort of revelation, something – he wasn't quite sure what. A cubby house maybe, amateurishly constructed out of fallen branches, a tent, a pile of books – something left behind.

Compare the following two versions of a sentence, both perfectly correct:

Just as a general guide a story ending rounds off, has a kind of dying fall to it, while a chapter ending rounds the chapter off but at the same time leads on.

Just as a general guide a story ending rounds off – has a kind of dying fall to it, while a chapter ending rounds the chapter off but at the same time leads on.

I much prefer the second version of this. The dash provides you with a longer or at least more noticeable pause, and draws attention to 'has a kind of dying fall'.

The double dash

I really like this device, but know that we have to be careful not to over-use it as a way of casually amplifying upon an idea in the sentence. Sometimes the sentence may require a tighter structure involving some other form of punctuation. The double dash is less controlled, less ordered than the bracket. Examples of its reasonable use might be these:

The sky was overcast – a sort of determined block white – and although the sun couldn't get through, it was suffusing the patch over the jetty with a yellowish stain.

As it came nearer too it seemed to be setting up an echo so that the whole hall – he seemed to be lying in an empty hall – echoed with his name.

The semicolon

Semicolons are useful when you want a strong pause but the parts of your sentence on each side of the pause are so strongly related that you don't want to start a new sentence. You can think of the semicolon as being a three-quarter pause between the comma (a half) and the full stop. You can use it in a sentence like this:

It reminded Gunno of a picture he had seen once of the entrance to a casino, where the roof rose, arching storeys high; the entrance was three or four times the normal height of such a room.

Or it is commonly used in a sentence which forms itself as a kind of list:

Multi-coloured umbrellas were going up – tilting at the sun; beach towels were being spread out; children were running everywhere.

Or again:

The blue wrens were the same, flitting and darting among the native cherries; the rosellas were the same sending their clear calls like sword blades through the clearings; the fresh smells of eucalypt were the same.

Its use is particularly appropriate here because repetition is being used in each of the three parts of the sentence. The semicolon helps to indicate this balance.

The colon
Colons are useful when you want to explain something or expand upon an idea or when you want to clarify what (in a general way) you have just said. They are also used to introduce a list or a quotation. Here are some examples:

He turned his bike and rode back to the start of the road that wound steeply down into the valley: the road that he had just climbed.
(clarification)

There had been something in the paper that morning that had made him think very clearly of Hugh: something to do with the date, was it?
(expansion)

They both laughed at that, though Gunno thought that he probably did mind: without the shelter of the gang, being with Jess was something different, something he wasn't sure he wanted, especially just now.
(explanation)

You will find that many novels will hover around one particular event or image: Robert Westall's *The Scarecrows on the three scarecrows in the field beside Simon's house,* Jane Gardam's *The* Summer After the Funeral *on the graveyard where Athene's father lies buried,* Penelope Lively's *The House in Norham* Gardens *on the image of snow.*
(an explanatory list)

   You could also use semicolons instead of commas here, and indeed, because of the length of each segment, I think that would be better.

And finally, from Sylvia Townsend Warner's *Letters*:

This miraculous summer still embraces us: the river flows gently and the moorhens converse and the enormous trout rise like explosions; we have never had such roses and the raspberries went on and on like Schubert and the figs are ripening.
(expansion)

Marks of elision
These are useful to mark a break in your character's speech or thought. What goes unsaid can be clearly enough indicated, as here, where the reader can guess at what is to follow: ' "Tell Wally I . . ." ' Or alternatively, may suggest or enforce a sense of mystery: 'And then in the paper that morning there had been something . . .'

These, then, are some of the main things to attend to when editing your work: repetition, sentence structure, pacing, general polishing and punctuation. What follow are a few additional pointers to keep in mind when looking at your story as a whole.

IS YOUR STORY LOGICAL?

Sometimes it is only when you start editing your story, thinking that it just needs a bit of light polishing, that you find major things wrong with it. If this happens you mustn't shut your eyes to the flaws. You may find that you haven't developed your story in a logical way.

   The House Guest involves a time slip, with Gunno going back two years to Hugh's time. I couldn't get the ending right until I came across something that I had written earlier about the story: 'I think the key to rendering it [the ending] properly is to remember that to Hugh Gunno is an ordinary boy; to Gunno Hugh is a kind of ghost'. It is important to keep up this kind of running commentary on your story and then, of course, not to lose track of your comments!

SALVAGING

If you have to substantially rewrite part of your story, but really like some of the material in it, see if you can salvage it in some way. Originally I made the plot of *The House Guest* depend on a bushfire, but I couldn't get it to work in the way that I needed it to in the story. The whole sequence had to come out. But I liked some of the description of the early stages of the fire as Gunno was riding his bike up the Clarendon road. So I managed to keep this in by turning it into a dust storm!

EXPANSIONS

Sometimes you may find that you have too many quiet parts in your story, all in the one place, unbroken by anything of greater interest. This is a challenge for you to decide if there is anything of potentially greater interest in your material, something that you have just summarised, perhaps. This happened to me in *The House Guest* when my eagle-eyed Penguin reader asked me to expand on the raid on Ross Road, to provide some action after too long a period of calm. What you do then is simply take the facts of the section that you have summarised, visualise them more fully, and develop them through action and dialogue. My original section was only a paragraph long:

He was talking about Ross Road, of course. Wally wasn't exaggerating: everything had gone wrong. It had been freezing yet the old woman was out in her garden; a furniture van had pulled up in the street; Siamese cats had yowled bitterly at them from two adjacent houses; and worst of all, in the third house, the one with the magnificent jacaranda out the front, they had come upon an elderly man asleep.

You can quite enjoy doing this work of expanding your material if you just regard it as an exercise. Similarly you can always shrink an episode if you find that it is over-extended and tedious, or perhaps repetitive of material elsewhere in the text.

LITTLE TIPS

Use of thoughts
Wandering around inside someone's thoughts is quite a good way of bringing in past incidents. (This is done in a very distinctive fashion in *Eleanor, Elizabeth* by Libby Gleeson.) You only *appear* to be wandering, however; actually you have something quite specific in mind.

Suspense
To check that a chapter is satisfactory in this regard, ask yourself how many questions are raised but not quite resolved in its course.

Making connections

Drop in early references to what will become important later in your story – as we found with the toolshed in Chapter 5. This will have the effect of preparing your reader, even if unconsciously, for what will happen, and will prevent elements in your story from seeming arbitrary.

A small example of what I mean is the reference to the fish tank in *Heffalump?*. My Penguin reader asked me to put in an apparently incidental reference to this earlier in the story, so that when Heffalump? falls into it, at the climax, it won't seem arbitrary. So I inserted this sentence about what Tiger sees from the front of a shelf in the toy cupboard:

Through the narrow slit in
front of his nose, all he could see were the
goldfish swimming placidly in their tank near
the window.

Ending in the right place

Be very careful that each chapter and indeed the story itself, ends in a strong place. It is amazing how many published novels seem to have gone on for one line too long. There seems to be a strong temptation to add just that one line of explanation which can seriously weaken the effect of your story. Watch out for that 'dying fall', and when you have achieved it, for goodness' sake, stop.

I do hope you will find that you enjoy editing your own work; it can make such a difference to a story if you are prepared to spend time on this. You will find that you improve critically too: you will become much better at looking at your story as if it were written by somebody else.

TRY THIS!

- Edit one of the stories which you wrote for the 'Try This!' section at the end of Chapter 4, keeping in mind the following headings: repetition, sentences and paragraphs that tail off, neatening what is clumsy, leaving out the obvious, being more specific, pacing and punctuation.

CHAPTER 8

Marketing Your Manuscript

CAN I GET SOMETHING PUBLISHED?

It is certainly difficult for a new writer to get something published: it would be foolish to think otherwise. Somehow you have to get yourself noticed, and it is well known that publishers have three piles for manuscripts: their own established authors, established authors from other publishers, and the 'slush' pile – that is, manuscripts from unknown authors.

Pile one gets top priority in terms of being looked at first. Pile two gets second priority, and I suppose the slush pile gets looked at when there is time free from other things. But do not despair. Publishers are not always so enthusiastic about some of the writers they already have; they are always hopeful (and the publishing business is very much one of hope) that one day they will find a wonderful new author in the slush pile. And remember too that most established authors have had to come up through it themselves, unless they have managed to get noticed in some other way. Janni Howker's magnificent, mature stories *Badger on the Barge* came up on Julia

MacRae's slush pile; Jane Gardam's *A Few Fair Days* on Hamish Hamilton's. That is why it is so important that you package your work well, that you have an arresting title, a marvellous opening and an exciting self-written blurb for your story. You want to give it the best possible chance.

And don't worry about your age. I know that the publisher at Angus & Robertson asked his editor to find out how old the writer was who had submitted *Something Special*, but this would only have been out of interest. (Actually, the writer *was* his editor, Jennifer Rowe, and about thirty-five, I think, at the time.) Publishers *will* bother about you, no matter what your age, if you are good enough. Lucy Boston was over sixty when she wrote *The Children of Green Knowe*, her first novel and now a classic. It is certainly quite common for novelists to be in their forties before they begin writing. Perhaps it has something to do with life experience, although I really think it has more to do with time. People with young families must really be struggling to find the time and energy to write, although, there again, people do manage it. Edith Nesbit, for example, surrounded by infant children, some of them the same age because some were her husband's but not her own, managed to write splendidly to help pay the many bills. (One such child was John Bland to whom *Five Children and It* is dedicated!) It all comes back to my earlier point: if you really want to do it you will overcome all obstacles; if you don't, then any excuse will seem sufficient.

And remember what I said earlier, and I will set this off as a separate paragraph to draw your attention to it yet again: at least at present, I really believe that your very best chance for publication lies in the area of story books for younger readers. (This may, of course, change at any time according to demand.) Even within this range there is plenty of opportunity for variety in terms of length and difficulty and nothing too restricting about the kinds of themes you may consider. If, of course, you have no interest in the area there is no point in pursuing this suggestion. Just write and keep on writing, in the area which attracts you most. However, it remains true that it is very difficult to break into the picture book area; the books are so expensive to produce, because of all the illustration and colour reproduction involved, that firms are publishing very few of these books, especially just now when the world market is depressed. The full-length novel is another difficult one to break into because of the sheer number and quality of the writers in this area. Story books for young children is still a growing area, with fewer strong writers. There seems to be much more chance here for a promising newcomer to be noticed and encouraged.

HAVE I GOT MY MANUSCRIPT INTO THE BEST POSSIBLE SHAPE?

Just do a last-minute check on your story before sending it off:

1. Does your manuscript fit, in length and difficulty, into one of the main marketable categories which we have identified?
Picture book texts
Story books for younger readers (6-10 years)
Novels (11+ through to adolescent)

2. Have you got the most out of your material? Have you developed it as far as you possibly can? Remember that the most common mistake in writing stories is to have too much material insufficiently developed.

3. Is your prose as polished as you can get it? Read it through yet again. (I know you are getting tired of it by now – so do we all.) Now read it aloud. Are there any lumps in the prose? If so, your sentence probably just needs rearranging. Is your meaning clear throughout or are some parts ambiguous, inexact or just plain murky?

4. Is your title the very best one for your story and for a publishing house? Is it the sort of title that prospective buyers would be sure to notice, like 'It Only Happens Once' and *Sooner or Later* by Sophie Masson?

5. Read through your opening paragraphs. Have you got straight into your story in such a way that the reader will be interested at once? Does it somehow sound as if you have come in on the middle of a situation, as though the characters were there before you started writing a story about them, and will still be there afterwards? If this were someone else's story, would you want to turn the page?

6. Does your story have a climax which then leads on to a resolution? Have you highlighted it sufficiently? Would a reader know that it is meant to be the high point, the turning point?

7. Check your ending. Is it as satisfying as you can make it? Have you rounded off all the information introduced

into the story? Will it leave the reader with a question that you should really have answered?

8. The last point to check is really the main and all-encompassing one: is this the very best that you can do with your material at this point in your writing career? If the answer is yes, then close your story, type a front page for it with the name of the story and your name and address clearly upon it, and prepare to send it off.

GIVING YOUR MANUSCRIPT
THE BEST POSSIBLE CHANCE

Packaging

Above all, you must make your manuscript look as if you *believe* in it. It's like everything else in life: if you don't believe in it and in yourself, no one else will. Type or word process it onto A4 paper, double spaced, with wide margins at the top, bottom and sides, and with a front page for it as described above. If it is a picture book text or short story you may just wish to hold the pages together with a paper-clip. If it is a novel you have written you could fasten the pages of each chapter together in the same way. Staples are acceptable too – indeed Angus & Robertson used to ask for the pages of each chapter to be fastened together, 'preferably stapled'. I believe some publishers, however, would rather have the pages loose, so it may well be safer, if you want to do anything at all, just to use large paper-clips.

You may type your name on each page of your

manuscript if you wish. Make sure the pages are numbered clearly. Send a letter with it to the editor of the firm you have chosen. Then put it in a padded envelope, address it neatly, remember to have it weighed at the post office, and send it off. The whole process is very exciting and terribly frightening. You will feel weak at the knees as you walk away from the slot where your package is now (only temporarily) at rest.

Choosing an appropriate publisher
Before this, of course, you have to decide which publisher to send your manuscript to. There is nothing to stop you sending it overseas, of course, to Julia MacRae in London, for example (for after all she is an Australian herself) but I really think that you have more chance in your own country. You may be able to experiment with overseas publishers later on, when you are established. Just think too of the enormous size of the population in Britain and in America, and think of all those manuscripts thudding onto the mats of publishers on any one day. In Australia we have more chance: so many people are involved in sport at the weekends that it must leave the field more open to us! There aren't nearly so many authors here and although the population is comparatively small (so that of course the reading public must be smaller too) you may find it encouraging to know that Australians buy more books per head of the population than do readers in either Britain or America. Indeed, as it is considered so lucrative, the Australian market is greatly sought after by these countries.

Choose, then, an Australian publisher. The two biggest firms, publishing the greatest number of titles are, I believe, Penguin Books Australia Ltd and

Collins/Angus & Robertson, the result of a merger. So you might like to try these first. Then again you might feel that you will have more chance with a smaller firm – Omnibus Books in Adelaide, for example, or The Five Mile Press in Melbourne. Check first to see what children's books the firm you fancy has been bringing out lately. There is no point in sending a work of fiction to a firm that has gone into educational books only, and not much point in sending a picture book text (especially when you are starting off) to someone who only brings one out every two years. But, so long as you keep things like that in mind, I really think you should send your books to the publisher you admire the most.

By now you have perhaps established quite a library of children's books. Use these now to find the addresses of the publishers you are interested in. You will find them on about the fourth page of a novel on the left-hand side where all the details of publication and printing are given.

The accompanying letter

You should, of course, (as I mentioned earlier) send a letter with your manuscript. Take the trouble to find out the name of the children's editor at your chosen firm and address it to her. I say 'her' not in any sexist sense but simply because most children's editors are women – although of course there are exceptions like Walter McVitty (of Walter McVitty Books) and Brian Cook at Collins. This will seem polite and will show the editor you mean business.

You don't need to say very much in the letter. Something like this will do:

Dear Suzanne Wilson, (a very nice, approachable Penguin editor)

I enclose for your consideration a story of approximately ten thousand words for young children. It is set in an inner suburb of Adelaide and is about an invalid child who becomes fascinated by the behaviour of a woman in his street who washes out the telephone box obsessively.

Yours sincerely,

Don't apologise for your story or say it is *you* who are obsessed by the idea of the woman, or that it is the first one you have written or that your own children love it. If you have had something published, for goodness' sake mention it, giving the year, the title and the publisher, for this will get you out of the slush pile automatically.

Perhaps I should add a postscript to this section. Since writing it, I have heard an editor say that if an accompanying letter is unusual it makes her more interested in the manuscript. So there you are. Formality may not always be best.

An exciting blurb

For a longish story or novel you will also have to include a synopsis of what your story is about. This should only be 100 words or so but it really is required. In its *Notes for Authors* pamphlet Angus & Robertson used to be quite firm about this and used to ask too for return postage.

In this synopsis you should simply outline the main drift of your story, making it sound as interesting as you can. What about this for our telephone box story?

A sick child, confined to the house, becomes fascinated by the behaviour of an elderly woman in his street, one of whose eccentricities is to wash out the local telephone box every morning. He studies her behaviour in all its variations, and comes to a frightening conclusion. But what he knows becomes too dreadful to tell, and who would believe the word, anyway, of a child and an invalid? Time is running out and there is only one person who could possibly help.

Obviously for a picture book it would be ridiculous to include a synopsis: in the time it took the editor to read it she could have read your text. But for story books or novels, do include one. With picture book texts, however, where the meaning of the text to some extent depends on how the illustrations are to be done, as would have been true of Gillian Rubinstein's *Dog In, Cat Out*, for example, it might be wise to include a statement about this.

SENDING YOUR MANUSCRIPT OFF

I would suggest that you only send your manuscript to one publisher at a time, except (perhaps) in the case of a picture book text, although even there I would hesitate. A publisher doesn't want to spend a lot of time on a story, wondering if it is marketable, thinking about a suitable illustrator, having meetings about it where perhaps four salaries are involved, only to find that some other publisher has taken the book. I mentioned the picture book text as perhaps being different, because it takes so little time to read, but then again, the publisher may have been spending time in contacting various illustrators. So really, I think you are better advised to send your manuscript to only one publisher at a time. One exception might be where you believe that you have written about something topical which will date quickly. In that case I would send it off to at least three publishers simultaneously, but say in the letter that you have done so and why.

What to expect

After a week or ten days you may hear from the publisher. Don't get too excited – the editor hasn't looked at your story yet. Someone from the office is simply writing to let you know that your manuscript has arrived. (I believe, though, that not all publishers do in fact acknowledge the receipt of manuscripts any more – they just get too many.) It is quite common to have to wait three to six months or even longer to hear about your actual story, so don't sit on the edge of your chair. If the publisher has had your manuscript for a very long time it may be that the firm is seriously considering it; if so, there should be some hint of this in the letter when it comes. It may be, of course, simply that they are terribly busy.

Waiting

This is when you really show your worth as a writer. You mustn't sit around brooding about the story that you have just written: get started on something fresh. This will protect you from being too upset if your manuscript is later rejected. It will help you to distance yourself by getting involved in a new story; writers always care most about the story they are working on at the moment. It makes previous titles recede in significance. It will give you fresh hope. Even if your first manuscript is rejected, you've got another one under way to try. You may even notice that you are getting better. This is all to the good, because if your manuscript is returned you will now be able to look at it more critically, in the light of your developing skills. Your skills will not develop if you shut up your typewriter and wait to see what will happen.

In the end though, you'll go out to the post-box and either there will be a letter from the publisher accepting your story, or your sad, slightly battered manuscript will have been returned to you. Let's look at the second situation first.

Rejection

Expect to feel awful, but bring your poor rejected child inside, and sit down and see what the publisher has to say about it. Keep telling yourself that nearly every published writer has had manuscripts returned, especially at the beginning of his or her career. Beatrix Potter tried six publishers, unsuccessfully, with *Peter Rabbit* – and then published it herself. Tolstoy tramped around unhappily with *War and Peace*, and William Golding's *Lord of the Flies* was in tatters by the time it got to the editor who finally published it. *Pride and Prejudice* languished in a drawer for years. It's the very fortunate and unusual person who gets something accepted straight away. So comfort yourself by thinking that it is a very common experience.

If it is a long letter, and they say a lot about your manuscript, you should feel (although you won't, just at this minute) very pleased, because someone in the publishing world believes that you are worth spending time on. They can see promise in your writing, and perhaps want to set you off in the right direction.

But I am afraid your letter is more likely to be quite brutally short. Perhaps if I could include here some of my early rejection slips to show you that we are all, or have been, and may be again (for there are no guarantees with writing) in the same boat. Here is the first one, but they get worse:

Thank you very much for sending us your two stories, A Lamb Like Alice *and* First Day. *We were most interested to read these but I am afraid we don't feel they quite fit our list.*

Interpretation: It's a kind, polite letter but they are not interested or encouraging at all. The polite brush-off.

Thank you for allowing us to see your manuscript of children's stories. The Children's Editor . . . has asked me to write and say that she feels your work is not suited to the style of publishing policy – that is to say we publish picture story books for which your texts are too long, and junior novels for which your texts are too short.

Interpretation: Again a very polite and kind letter, and longer this time. (You get to be grateful for very small mercies!) But they are still not really interested, are they? 'Not suited to the style of publishing policy' is just a polite form of words to say they don't want your story – I don't think it has any further significance than this. You do wonder why they don't try reading the long picture story book text as a junior novel, but perhaps this is an uncharitable thought. They are probably actually trying to be helpful and that is why we have to be grateful for a longer letter. They are saying that what I have written is not within the marketable categories of children's books, and while this is a serious criticism, it is one that something can be done about. So on the whole, this is a better rejection letter than the first. It gives me some advice in indicating how I can make my stories more marketable.

Your writing is smoothly produced, but sentimental, and has a sameness and predictability that deprive it of impact.

Interpretation: Perhaps it doesn't need any! This is the sort of rejection notice that makes you want to rush outside and do something odd like clean out telephone boxes. It's very hurtful. At least I found it so. Here I was writing moving stories, I thought, and they are dismissed, ridiculed even, as being sentimental. And they are not only sentimental, but what is worse, boring.

You might wonder how I had the hide to go on writing after that one. Still, as I have said, if you want to write and be published, you have to believe in yourself and expect set-backs. Even established writers are always getting set-backs of one kind or another.

This was the most hurtful of my rejection slips and yet, in the long run, the most helpful. I asked a writer friend what you did if your stories were sentimental, and he said, well, it's just a question of cutting. Just cut it back. That made me feel a lot calmer; if I were overdoing it, then all I had to do was cut. It was just a question of technique, not a defect in my psyche. The other charge was more serious; obviously my story-telling skills were in pretty bad shape. A dose of Ruth Rendell was clearly in order.

The main thing is not to feel as if *you* have been rejected, as if there is something wrong with you if you have written stories which are described as being sentimental and boring. As I have said before, since our stories really present a map of our minds, of what we care about the most, it is very hard not to take rejection in a very personal way. Nevertheless we have to try.

Forget about how you feel. Remember that all editors have different approaches, have different likes and dislikes. Inspect your manuscript and see if it still looks clean and tidy. If not, then get out a fresh photocopy. (Always keep several copies of each story, won't you?) Find another padded envelope and send it off to the second publisher on your list, and then forget about it. If it gets returned, then repeat the process.

But if a story gets rejected by four to six children's editors, especially if they all say the same sort of thing, it may be the time to reread the story and see if you can improve it. Or, if you can't bear to do that, put it away in a drawer and see if you can't do better with a new idea. But don't, in a fit of pique or desperation, destroy your story. One day you may know exactly how to market it.

Rejection slips will be different, and will affect you differently, once a publisher has already accepted something of yours. The editor may then say, well we didn't feel so enthusiastic about this one – we didn't feel it had the pace and interest of *Wombat's Hole*, for example. They will only run your new story down by praising up your old story, which they *have* published, and although this isn't pleasant either, since you are probably more attached to your new story than to *Wombat's Hole*, you will get over it more quickly. And after all, when you think about it, you don't want to have a story published which is less than your best.

Acceptance
At first you will feel that this is the happiest day in your life: you are to be an author, just, perhaps, as once you

were to be a parent. The thrill is a little similar. You are
to see your idea in book form with your name on the
cover. A dream come true. But happiness tends to be
tempered, and I think you may find that this is so now.

Although your story has been accepted, no contract
can be drawn up until an illustrator has been
found – unless it is a novel you have written for the 11
age group or older. In this case an illustrator is only
needed to do the cover, and the contract can be drawn
up without waiting for that. This waiting will tend to
make you uneasy, but it needn't really. It is simply
standard practice.

It is customary to be paid an advance for a book, the
amount depending on what kind of book it is and how
well known you are, I suspect. For a new writer with a
small print run (where the publisher is taking a greater
risk) the advance may be quite a small one; a big-name
author, on the other hand, will get a much more
substantial advance because the publisher knows that
sales are assured. Advances are paid in instalments, often
in this way: one third on the signing of the contract, one
third on typesetting and one third on publication. This
money will be deducted from your first royalty cheque.

Royalties are paid twice a year, at the end of March
and September, to cover sales for the preceding six
months. Author and illustrator share a 10% royalty: this
means that for every book sold the author and illustrator
get a tenth of the retail price except for book club sales,
like those of Ashton Scholastic, for which the royalty is
much lower.

With picture books it is usual for the royalty to be
divided equally between author and illustrator, although
if the illustrator is much better known than the author,
or if the illustrations have taken years to do (this

sometimes happens) the publisher may negotiate for a
bigger slice to go to the illustrator. Illustrators often feel
that it is unfair for the author to get as much as they do
since the text may have taken only a matter of weeks to
do, and the illustrations months or even longer. But I
think it *is* fair since the idea is usually the author's, and
no idea, no picture book.

With story books like the Young Puffins a likely
distribution is 60% to the author and 40% to the
illustrator, but this is completely flexible: the split could
be 50/50 or even 75/25. With novels you may get the
whole 10%, with the illustrator being paid outright for
the cover. If the novel is a shorter one, however, with
say ten or more illustrations, the royalty may be divided
80% to the author and 20% to the illustrator. Again this
may vary considerably.

You can see then that unless a book sells a tremendous
number of copies it is unlikely that you can give up your
steady job or buy a Jaguar. Fortunes are rarely made
with books, and it is best to see the money as a pleasant
extra, not as a substitute for more gainful employment.
Not that I think this is necessarily a bad thing. To crouch
permanently over a typewriter or to peer endlessly into
a screen seems a rather lonely and limiting way of
earning a living. It would also be extremely draining.

EDITORIAL HELP

But the waiting for the contract to be signed and for the
book actually to come out (which may not happen for a
year or more) is nothing compared to what usually
upsets the beginning author most: the editorial changes

which the publisher wants to make in the manuscript. It is understandable that the writer who has spent hours and hours polishing a story should resist and indeed resent the efforts of others to improve it. Nevertheless we have to learn to co-operate with our editors. After all, at last we have found someone who believes we can write and all the editor wants is for the manuscript to go out into the marketplace in the best possible shape.

This doesn't mean that we have to slavishly accept every suggested change, but we should consider each one carefully. Editors have considerable experience with manuscripts and can often put their finger on something that is wrong. They may not know how to correct it, or they may try to correct it in the wrong way, but the mere fact that something worries them about the story at a certain point should make us consider their opinion very seriously.

Authors obviously give publishers a hard time, as you become aware when you read Jennifer Rowe's *Murder by the Book*, set in a publishing firm at the time of an amalgamation. (Jennifer Rowe, as you may remember, worked for many years as chief editor at Angus & Robertson's.) A party is being given for their authors who are all fairly strange and difficult in their various ways. But the worst of all turns out to be the children's writer . . .

The relationship between author and editor is a very important one: if they can work well together they will produce a far better manuscript than the author could have achieved alone. If you find that you are not at ease with your editor, indeed that you don't trust her judgement, then get the current book published with the firm but look for another one, with a more congenial editor, for your next. Be wary though: be very sure first that it isn't your fault. We all tend to be very sensitive about our writing and resentful of criticism.

Unfortunately too, editors tend to disappear. One minute the editor you really like is there, calm and friendly and ready to take an extravagant interest in your story or idea, and the next, it seems, she has gone. They leave to have babies, to move to other firms, to freelance perhaps, to take other jobs. Maybe the writers have got too much for them! It is also not a well-paid job considering how important it is, and how skilled and demanding the work. I always think of editors as being the custodians of the language.

Writers are often difficult and prickly and editors may never really guess how dependent writers become on them. I think it is a relationship where the writer needs the editor more than vice versa, and perhaps it is this imbalance which at times causes trouble. Writers need encouragement when they are being particularly unsuccessful, when they are sitting in dull rooms with blank minds in front of equally blank screens. If an editor guesses this, and rings up at one of these bad times, this may be sufficient to pull the writer out of a slump.

The main thing to remember is that stories can be changed: they are not carved in granite. If you try to think back to when you were composing your story, you must remember times when your idea stood at a sort of crossroads and could have been developed in more than one direction. The same with your words; you were perfectly happy then to change the words around until your meaning became clearer or the sentence flowed more smoothly. Try mentally to get back to that time when your story was in a fluid state; try to regard it as still fluid when you have your chats either in person or over the phone or in writing with your editor. With some stories you will need more editorial help than others. And remember, publishers often decide to do stories because of their *potential*, not because of what is already there. They can see that the material is a bit rough and chaotic but they have the experience to see that it can be knocked into shape. In other words, they are not choosing our stories because they think they are perfectly crafted already. They expect to have input. And remember, it is *their* money, and *their* risk.

One story that I needed a lot of help with was about a boy's relationship with a wild Australian duck, (*The Black Duck* which I mentioned previously). I'm not saying that I realised I needed all this help, or that I was always particularly gracious about receiving it. The story was imperfect in many of the usual ways. I kept changing the viewpoint from that of the little boy in the story to that of the adults, so that a lot of the impetus was lost and it would have been hard for a reader to become sufficiently involved. I totally skipped, left out, the climax, letting it fall sadly in between two chapters. I rushed the ending, no doubt feeling exhausted, once I got to it, by the whole exercise. Apart from all that, the beginning was very slow and tentative and the title, *Squeak Toy*, although one I particularly liked, was thought by the publishers to be misleading. They felt that it sounded as if the story were for readers younger than we intended. You would wonder at a publisher wanting to do such a story at all, with so much wrong with it, but I suppose they believed in me enough to think that I could rewrite it. There was no contract, of course, until I had done so. The wise publisher waits to have the story as he or she wants it before signing a contract and parting with money. And this story took a very long time to shape.

At first I struggled a bit at the thought of all these changes. I didn't think the story was all that bad as it was. But even when I became convinced that my astute reader had put her usual finger on the holes in the story, I still resisted altering it. I didn't say anything about all this resistance of course, except passively, perhaps, by silence and by not doing anything. One tries to keep these inner turmoils from the publisher as much as possible.

I resisted altering it because I wasn't sure that I could: I had written the story in the best way I knew how to, and I was afraid that I wasn't a good enough writer to change it. But Julie Watts at Penguin coaxed me along with it, showing me, as my friend had done earlier about the problem of sentimentality, that it was all simply a question of technique. All I had to do this time was change the point of view in a few scenes and insert an extra scene for the climax, which in context, she said kindly and optimistically, should write itself.

So I got out the reader's report again which talked of the 'vast anticlimax' at the centre of the story, about how I had stepped back 'from the realities of the situation', and about the story's unfortunate shifts in point of view. And I sat down and slowly, painfully, but with growing heart, because I could see that it was getting better, I rewrote the story.

THE PUBLISHER'S READER

I don't think I have said very much previously about the function of a publisher's reader in the complicated process of book production. Publishers send manuscripts to their readers to see if they will recommend publication. I don't believe publishers bother with this part of the process unless they are seriously considering the title concerned. If they are completely sure that they want to publish, I don't suppose they bother either. These readers have considerable experience in the children's book world: perhaps they run children's bookshops, for example, or work as children's librarians.

These reports will be sent to you if the reader recommends publication, subject to certain changes. The reports are most useful – you will find that they give you considerable help. They will also supply you with much encouragement, because the reader will say what she or he likes about the story and about you as a writer. And it is so wonderful, wandering in the desert of our imperfectly realised stories, to receive praise.

I wrote a story once called *A Sea Change* which I mean to get back to one day and finish. Why I mention it is that, although the reader did not recommend publication, she said something about it which helped to give me permanent faith in myself as a writer.

SHARING YOUR JOY

I think it is wise not to say too much about the success of your story outside your family. Perhaps we tend to be too thrilled about it, and so get people's backs up. In any case you cannot expect other people to be as excited as you are about it. It is also true that being published is a very common ambition, and some people may tend to feel a little bit cheated when someone they know gets published before they do. Many people, too, feel that it is a rather odd thing to do to write for children. 'For *children*,' they say, obviously wondering when you are going to do some proper writing. Just be very grateful for any friends or family who are genuinely pleased and take an interest in your success. Treasure them.

AN EMOTIONAL BUSINESS

I hope too that I have somehow managed to stress throughout what an emotional business writing is. If you move from elation to despair you must not think that this is abnormal: writing creates its own highs and lows. There is not much that you can do about this except perhaps to recognise that it is so, and to handle it as best you can. You will get better at it with time. Just remember that you are particularly sensitive on your writing side; we are all very vulnerable there, as we are in fact revealing our personalities quite clearly, even if in apparently indirect ways. Writing is one of the activities that will give us a great deal of happiness, but at times too, a fair share of misery.

Well, it only remains for me to wish you all the very best with your writing, and to ask you a question if I may. (Please be kind.) How much chance do you think I have of getting my telephone box story published?

P. S. If you're still wondering(!) about who wrote the lovely passage quoted in Chapter 6 about the fowls doing *their* writing (even if only in the dust), it was William Mayne (from *Gideon Ahoy!*).

Bibliography

PICTURE BOOKS

Barbalet, Margaret and Tanner, Jane (illust.) *The Wolf* Penguin Books Australia, Melbourne, 1991.

Browne, Anthony *Willy the Wimp* Methuen Children's Books, London, 1986.

Carle, Eric *The Very Hungry Caterpillar* Hamish Hamilton, London, 1970.

Clement, Rod *Counting on Frank* Collins/Angus & Robertson, Sydney, 1990.

Cole, Joanna and Degen, Bruce (illust.) *The Magic Schoolbus at the Waterworks* Scholastic Inc., New York, 1986.

Coleridge, Ann and Harvey, Roland (illust.) *The Friends of Emily Culpepper* The Five Mile Press, Victoria, 1983.

Croser, Josephine and Carter, Donni (illust.) *Tiddycat* Collins Publishers Australia, Sydney, 1989.

Dahl, Roald and Blake, Quentin (illust.) *Revolting Rhymes* Penguin Books, Harmondsworth,1984.

Denton, Terry *Felix and Alexander* Oxford University Press, Melbourne, 1985.

Dutton, Geoffrey and Smith, Craig (illust.) *The Prowler* William Collins, Sydney, 1982.

Flack, Marjorie and Wiese, Kurt *The Story About Ping* Penguin Books, Harmondsworth, 1968. (First published in 1935 by The Bodley Head.)

Fox, Mem and Vivas, Julie (illust.) *Possum Magic* Omnibus Books, Adelaide, 1983.

Gag, Wanda *Millions of Cats* Penguin Books, Harmondsworth, 1976. (First published in 1929 by Faber & Faber.)

Hoban, Russell and Hoban, Lillian (illust.) *The Stone Doll of Sister Brute* The Macmillan Company, New York, 1968.

Holl, Adelaide and Duvoisin, Roger (illust.) *The Rain Puddle* The Bodley Head, London, 1966.

Hughes, Shirley *Dogger* William Collins, London, 1979.

Hunt, Nan and Smith, Craig (illust.) *Whistle Up the Chimney* William Collins, Sydney, 1981.

Hutchins, Pat *Rosie's Walk* Penguin Books, Harmondsworth, 1970.

Mattingley, Christobel and Smith, Craig (illust.) *Black Dog* William Collins, Sydney, 1979.

Mayer, Mercer *There's an Alligator Under My Bed* J. M. Dent, Melbourne, 1987.

Murphy, Jill *Five Minutes' Peace* Walker Books, London, 1986.

Nilsson, Eleanor and Argent, Leanne (illust.) *Tatty* Omnibus Books, Adelaide, 1985.

Nilsson, Eleanor and Smith, Craig (illust.) *Parrot Fashion* Omnibus Books, Adelaide, 1983.

Oakley, Graham *Henry's Quest* Macmillan Children's Books, London, 1986.

Potter, Beatrix *The Tale of Jemima Puddle-Duck* Frederick Warne, London, 1908.

Potter, Beatrix *The Tale of Peter Rabbit* Frederick Warne, London, 1902.

Rubinstein, Gillian and James, Ann (illust.) *Dog In, Cat Out* Omnibus Books, Adelaide, 1991.

Sendak, Maurice *Where the Wild Things Are* Penguin Books, Harmondsworth, 1970.

Steiner, Jörg and Müller, Jörg (illust.) *The Bear Who Wanted to Stay a Bear* Andersen Press, London, 1986.

Wagner, Jenny and Brooks, Ron (illust.) *John Brown, Rose and the Midnight Cat* Penguin Books Australia, Melbourne, 1977.

Wild, Margaret and Harris, Wayne (illust.) *A Bit of Company* Ashton Scholastic, Sydney, 1991.

Wild, Margaret and Tanner, Jane (illust.) *There's a Sea in My Bedroom* Thomas Nelson Australia, Melbourne, 1984.

Wild, Margaret and Vivas, Julie (illust.) *Let the Celebrations Begin!* Omnibus Books, Adelaide, 1991.

Wild, Margaret and Vivas, Julie (illust.) *The Very Best of Friends* Margaret Hamilton Books, Sydney, 1989.
Wilhelm, Hans *I'll Always Love You* Hodder & Stoughton, Sydney, 1986.

STORY BOOKS

Ashley, Bernard *Dinner Ladies Don't Count* (includes *Linda's Lie*) Penguin Books, Harmondsworth, 1984.
Bond, Michael *A Bear Called Paddington* William Collins, London, 1958.
Dann, Max *Adventures with My Worst Best Friend* Oxford University Press, Melbourne, 1982.
Fine, Anne *The Country Pancake* Mammoth, London, 1991.
Gardam, Jane *A Few Fair Days* Penguin Books, Harmondsworth, 1974.
Gardam, Jane *Bridget and William* Julia MacRae Books, London, 1981.
Godden, Rumer *The Mousewife* published in *Mouse Time* Methuen Children's Books, London, 1984.
Hoban, Russell *Dinner At Alberta's* Penguin Books, Harmondsworth, 1980.
Hooke, Nina Warner *The Snow Kitten* Penguin Books, Harmondsworth, 1978.
Hughes, Ted *How the Whale Became and Other Stories* Penguin Books, Harmondsworth, 1971.
Jennings, Paul *The Cabbage Patch Fib* Penguin Books Australia, Melbourne, 1988.
Kenward, Jean *Ragdolly Anna* Penguin Books, Harmondsworth, 1984.
Kidd, Diana *Onion Tears* William Collins, Sydney, 1989.
Kipling, Rudyard *Just So Stories* Piccolo Books, 1986. (First published in 1902 by Macmillan.)
Klein, Robin and Lester, Alison (illust.) *Thing* Oxford University Press, Melbourne, 1982.

Klein, Robin and Wilcox, Cathy (illust.) *Boris and Borsch* Allen
& Unwin, Sydney, 1990.
Klein, Robin *The Enemies* Angus & Robertson, Sydney, 1985.
Lurie, Morris *The 27th Annual African Hippopotamus Race*
Penguin Books Australia, Melbourne, 1977.
Mark, Jan *The Dead Letter Box* Penguin Books,
Harmondsworth, 1983.
Mark, Jan *The Twig Thing* Penguin Books, Harmondsworth,
1990.
Mattingley, Christobel and Mullins, Patricia (illust.) *Rummage*
Angus & Robertson, Sydney, 1981.
Mattingley, Christobel *Duck Boy* Penguin Books,
Harmondsworth, 1985.
Milne, A.A. *Winnie-the-Pooh* Methuen Children's Books,
London, 1972. (First published in 1926 by Methuen & Co.)
Nilsson, Eleanor *A Lamb Like Alice* Angus & Robertson,
Sydney, 1990.
Nilsson, Eleanor *Heffalump?* Penguin Books Australia,
Melbourne, 1986.
Nilsson, Eleanor *Pomily's Wish* Penguin Books Australia,
Melbourne, 1987.
Nilsson, Eleanor *The 89th Kitten* Angus & Robertson, Sydney,
1987.
Nilsson, Eleanor *The Black Duck* Penguin Books Australia,
Melbourne, 1990.
Odgers, Sally Farrell *The Follow Dog* Omnibus Books,
Adelaide, 1990.
Pearce, Philippa 'Black Eyes' in *Black Eyes* Pepper Press,
Leeds, 1981.
Peguero, Leone and Peters, Shirley (illust.) *Mervyn's Revenge*
Margaret Hamilton Books, Sydney, 1990.
Phipson, Joan *Hide Till Daytime* Penguin Books,
Harmondsworth, 1979.
Rodda, Emily *Pigs Might Fly* Angus & Robertson, 1986.
Rodda, Emily *Something Special* Angus & Robertson, Sydney,
1984.

Rodda, Emily *The Best-kept Secret* Angus & Robertson, Sydney, 1988.

Rubinstein, Gillian and Smith, Craig (illust.) *Squawk and Screech* Omnibus Books, Adelaide, 1991.

Rubinstein, Gillian *Melanie and the Night Animal* Omnibus Books, Adelaide, 1988.

Tomlinson, Jill *The Owl Who Was Afraid of the Dark* Penguin Books, Harmondsworth, 1973.

White, E. B. *Charlotte's Web* Penguin Books, Harmondsworth, 1963. (First published in 1952 by Hamish Hamilton.)

NOVELS AND SHORT STORIES

Aldridge, James *The Broken Saddle* Penguin Books, Harmondsworth, 1984.

Boston, Lucy *The Children of Green Knowe* Penguin Books, Harmondsworth, 1975. (First published in 1954 by Faber & Faber.)

Burnett, Frances Hodgson *The Secret Garden* Penguin Books, Harmondsworth, 1951. (First published in 1911 by William Heinemann.)

Byars, Betsy *The Eighteenth Emergency* Penguin Books, Harmondsworth, 1976.

Carmody, Isobelle *The Farseekers* Penguin Books Australia, Melbourne, 1990.

Christopher, John *The Guardians* Penguin Books, Harmondsworth, 1973.

Cormier, Robert *The Bumblebee Flies Anyway* William Collins, London, 1983.

Crew, Gary *Strange Objects* Mammoth Australia, Melbourne, 1991.

Fine, Anne *The Granny Project* Mammoth, London, 1990.

Fitzhugh, Louise *Harriet the Spy* William Collins, London, 1975.

Gardam, Jane *A Long Way from Verona* Penguin Books, Harmondsworth, 1973.

Gardam, Jane *Bilgewater* Hamish Hamilton, London, 1976
Gardam, Jane *The Summer After the Funeral* Hamish Hamilton, London, 1973.
Garner, Alan *Red Shift* William Collins, London, 1973.
Gleeson, Libby *Eleanor, Elizabeth* Angus & Robertson, Sydney, 1984.
Harding, Lee *Displaced Person* Penguin Books Australia, Melbourne, 1981.
Harding, Lee *Waiting for the End of the World* Penguin Books Australia, Melbourne, 1985.
Howker, Janni *Badger on the Barge* Julia MacRae Books, 1984.
Jennings, Paul *Unbelievable!* Penguin Books Australia, Melbourne, 1987.
Kelleher, Victor *Del-Del* Random House Australia, Sydney, 1991.
Kelleher, Victor *Master of the Grove* Penguin Books, Harmondsworth, 1983.
Kelleher, Victor *Taronga* Penguin Books Australia, Melbourne, 1988.
Klein, Robin *Halfway Across the Galaxy and Turn Left* Penguin Books Australia, Melbourne, 1985.
Klein, Robin *Hating Alison Ashley* Penguin Books Australia, Melbourne, 1984.
Klein, Robin *People Might Hear You* Penguin Books Australia, Melbourne, 1983.
Le Guin, Ursula *A Wizard of Earthsea* Penguin Books, Harmondsworth, 1971.
Lively, Penelope *A House Inside Out* Penguin Books, Harmondsworth, 1989.
Lively, Penelope *The Ghost of Thomas Kempe* Pan Books, London, 1975.
Lively, Penelope *The House in Norham Gardens* Pan Books, London, 1977.
Macdonald, Caroline *The Eye Witness* Hodder & Stoughton, Sydney, 1991.
Macdonald, Caroline *The Lake at the End of the World* Penguin Books Australia, Melbourne, 1989.

Mahy, Margaret *The Changeover* Methuen Children's Books, London, 1985.

Mahy, Margaret *The Haunting* J. M. Dent & Sons, London, 1982.

Mark, Jan *Handles* Kestrel, Penguin Books, Harmondsworth, 1983.

Mark, Jan *Nothing to be Afraid Of* Penguin Books, Harmondsworth, 1982.

Mark, Jan *Thunder and Lightnings* Penguin Books, Harmondsworth, 1978.

Mark, Jan *Under the Autumn Garden* Penguin Books, Harmondsworth, 1980.

Marsden, John *So Much to Tell You* . . . Walter McVitty Books, NSW, 1988.

Masson, Sophie 'It Only Happens Once' in *After Dark* Omnibus Books, Adelaide, 1988.

Masson, Sophie *Sooner or Later* University of Queensland Press, 1991.

Mayne, William *A Swarm in May* Oxford University Press, London, 1955.

Mayne, William *Gideon Ahoy!* Penguin Books, Harmondsworth, 1989.

Mayne, William *It* Penguin Books, Harmondsworth, 1980.

Mayne, William *No More School* Penguin Books, Harmondsworth, 1968.

Mayne, William *The Jersey Shore* Hamish Hamilton, London, 1973.

Nesbit, Edith *Five Children and It* Penguin Books, Harmondsworth, 1959. (First published in 1902 by T. Fisher Unwin.)

Nilsson, Eleanor *The House Guest* Penguin Books Australia, Melbourne, 1991.

Norton, Mary *The Borrowers* Penguin Books, Harmondsworth, 1958.

Park, Ruth *Playing Beatie Bow* Thomas Nelson Australia, Melbourne, 1980.

Pearce, Philippa *A Dog So Small* Penguin Books, Harmondsworth, 1964.

Pearce, Philippa *Tom's Midnight Garden* Oxford University Press, London, 1970. (First published in 1958.)

Phipson, Joan *The Boundary Riders* Penguin Books, Harmondsworth, 1965.

Phipson, Joan *The Cats* Pan Books, London, 1978.

Rubinstein, Gillian *Answers to Brut* Omnibus Books, Adelaide, 1988.

Rubinstein, Gillian *Beyond the Labyrinth* Hyland House, Melbourne, 1988.

Rubinstein, Gillian *Space Demons* Omnibus Books, Adelaide, 1986.

Southall, Ivan *Bread and Honey* Penguin Books, Harmondsworth, 1972.

Southall, Ivan *Josh* Penguin Books, Harmondsworth, 1973.

Spence, Eleanor *A Candle for Saint Antony* Oxford University Press, Melbourne, 1977.

Thiele, Colin *Blue Fin* Rigby Limited, Adelaide, 1969.

Tolkien, J. R. R. *The Hobbit* George Allen & Unwin, London, 1966. (First published 1937.)

Turner, Ethel *Seven Little Australians* Ward Lock, Sydney, 1976. (First published in 1894.)

Voigt, Cynthia *Dicey's Song* William Collins, London, 1984.

Westall, Robert *The Scarecrows* Penguin Books, Harmondsworth, 1983.

Wrightson, Patricia *A Little Fear* Hutchinson Australia, Melbourne, 1983.

Wrightson, Patricia *Down to Earth* Penguin Books, Harmondsworth, 1972.

ADULT NOVELS

Austen, Jane *Emma* Penguin Books, Harmondsworth, 1981. (First published in 1816.)

Austen, Jane *Mansfield Park* Chatto & Windus, London, 1975. (First published in 1814.)

Brookner, Anita *Hotel du Lac* Jonathan Cape, London, 1984.

BIBLIOGRAPHY

Drabble, Margaret *The Millstone* Penguin Books, Harmondsworth, 1977.
Eliot, George *Middlemarch* W.W. Norton & Co., New York, 1977. (First published 1871–1872.)
Huxley, Aldous *Brave New World* Penguin Books, Harmondsworth, 1969.
Orwell, George *1984* Penguin Books, Harmondsworth, 1970.
Rendell, Ruth *Heartstones* Arrow Books, Century Hutchinson, 1988.
Rendell, Ruth *Live Flesh* Arrow Books, Century Hutchinson, 1986.
Vine, Barbara *A Dark-Adapted Eye* Penguin Books, Harmondsworth, 1986.

HANDBOOKS AND CRITICAL WORKS

Aiken, Joan *The Way to Write for Children* Elm Tree Books, London, 1982.
Nieuwenhuizen, Agnes *Good Books for Teenagers* Mandarin, Melbourne, 1992.
Nieuwenhuizen, Agnes *No Kidding* Pan Macmillan Publishers Australia, NSW, 1991.
Nimon, Maureen 'Living with Ourselves: Recent Australian Science Fiction for Children and Young People' *The Children's Literature Association Quarterly*, Vol.15, No.4, Winter, 1990 pp. 185–189.
Strunk, William, Jr. and White, E. B. *The Elements of Style* Macmillan, 1959. (First edition.)
Whitney, Phyllis A. *Writing Juvenile Stories and Novels* The Writer, Inc., Boston, 1986 reprint. (First published 1976.)

Acknowledgements

For permission to reprint the extracts in this book, acknowledgement is made to the following:

Joan Aiken: *The Way to Write for Children* reproduced by courtesy of Hamish Hamilton Ltd; 'Happy Ever After' from *Reading Time* (October, 1980).
James Aldridge: *The Broken Saddle* © 1982 James Aldridge, published in the UK by Walker Books Ltd.
Bernard Ashley: *Linda's Lie* text © 1982 Bernard Ashley, illustrations © 1982 Janet Duchesne, published in the UK by Walker Books Ltd.
Nina Bawden: 'A Dead Pig and My Father' in *Children's Literature in Education*, Vol. 14 (1974), pp. 4 and 13.
Eric Carle: *The Very Hungry Caterpillar* copyright © Eric Carle, 1969, published by Hamish Hamilton Children's Books.
A. Coleridge: *The Friends of Emily Culpepper* by A. Coleridge and R. Harvey (illustrator) copyright © Roland Harvey Studios. Reproduced by kind permission.
Roald Dahl: 'The Three Little Pigs' from *Revolting Rhymes*, published by Jonathan Cape Ltd and Penguin Books Ltd.
Margaret Drabble: *The Millstone*, published by Weidenfeld and Nicolson publishers, J. M. Dent.

Max Fatchen: *Songs For My Dog and Other People* (Viking Kestrel, 1980) copyright © Max Fatchen, 1980. Reproduced by permission of Penguin Books Ltd.

Anne Fine: *The Granny Project* published by Methuen Children's Books.

Louise Fitzhugh: *Harriet the Spy* published by Victor Gollancz Ltd.

Marjorie Flack: *The Story About Ping* by permission of The Random Century Group Ltd.

Mem Fox: *Possum Magic* (1983) published by Omnibus Books.

Wanda Gag: *Millions of Cats* published by Faber & Faber Ltd.

Jane Gardam: *Bridget and William* published by Julia MacRae Books, by permission of David Higham Associates Ltd.

Leon Garfield: 'Bookmaker and Punter' in *The Thorny Paradise*, ed. Edward Blishen, Penguin Books Ltd, Harmondsworth (1975), p. 81.

Russell Hoban: *The Stone Doll of Sister Brute* by permission of Aitken & Stone Ltd.

Adelaide Holl: *The Rain Puddle* by permission of The Random Century Group Ltd.

Janni Howker: *Badger on the Barge* © 1984 Janni Howker, published in the UK by Walker Books Ltd.

Paul Jennings: 'Pink Bow Tie' in *Unbelievable!*, published by Penguin Books Australia Ltd.

Victor Kelleher: *Del-Del*, reproduced by permission of the author.

Jean Kenward: *Ragdolly Anna* copyright © Yorkshire Television, reproduced by permission of Yorkshire Television Enterprises Ltd.

Rudyard Kipling: 'The Elephant's Child' in *Just So Stories* reproduced by permission of Macmillan London.

Robin Klein: *Hating Alison Ashley*, published by Penguin Books Australia Ltd.

C. S. Lewis: 'On Three Ways of Writing for Children' in *Children and Literature*, edited by Virginia Haviland. Scott, Foresman and Company: Glenview, Illinois (1973), pp. 232 and 233.

Penelope Lively: *A House Inside Out* (1989) by permission of Scholastic Publications Ltd.

Margaret Mahy: *The Changeover*, J. M. Dent publishers.

Walter de la Mare: permission to reproduce extracts from 'The Truants' and 'Words' by Walter de la Mare given by The Literary Trustees of Walter de la Mare and The Society of Authors as their representative.

Jan Mark: *The Dead Letter Box* copyright © Jan Mark, 1982, published by Hamish Hamilton Children's Books. *Handles* (Viking Kestrel, 1983) copyright © Jan Mark, 1983; *Nothing to be Afraid Of* (Viking Kestrel, 1980) copyright © Jan Mark, 1977/1980; *Thunder and Lightnings* (Viking Kestrel, 1976) copyright © Jan Mark, 1976; *Under the Autumn Garden* (Viking Kestrel, 1977) copyright © Jan Mark, 1977; reproduced by permission of Penguin Books Ltd.

John Marsden: *So Much To Tell You . . .* published by Walter McVitty Books.

Sophie Masson: 'It Only Happens Once' in *After Dark* (1988) published by Omnibus Books.

Christobel Mattingley: *Duck Boy* by permission of Collins/Angus & Robertson Publishers.

Mercer Mayer: *There's an Alligator Under My Bed* copyright © 1987 by Mercer Mayer. Used by permission of Dial Books for Young Readers, a division of Penguin Books USA Inc.

William Mayne: *Gideon Ahoy!* (Viking Kestrel, 1987) copyright © William Mayne, 1987. Reproduced by permission of Penguin Books Ltd; *It* (published by Hamish Hamilton), *No More School* (published by Penguin Books) and *A Swarm in May* (published by Oxford University Press) by permission of David Higham Associates Ltd.

A. A. Milne: *Winnie the Pooh* published by Methuen Children's Books.

Philippa Pearce: *A Dog So Small* (Puffin Books, 1964) copyright © Philippa Pearce, 1962. Reproduced by permission of Penguin Books Ltd.

Beatrix Potter: *The Tailor of Gloucester* copyright © Frederick Warne & Co., 1903, 1987; *The Tale of Jemima Puddle-Duck* copyright © Frederick Warne & Co., 1908, 1987; *The Tale of Peter Rabbit* copyright © Frederick Warne & Co., 1902, 1987, all reproduced by permission of Frederick Warne & Co.

Ruth Rendell: *Heart Stones* published by Hutchinson, by permission of The Random Century Group Ltd.

Emily Rodda: *The Best-kept Secret*, by permission of Collins/Angus & Robertson Publishers.

Gillian Rubinstein: *Melanie and the Night Animal* (1988), *Space Demons* (1986) and *Squawk and Screech* (1991) published by Omnibus Books.

Maurice Sendak: *Where the Wild Things Are*, by permission of The Random Century Group Ltd.

Hugh Shelley: *Arthur Ransome*, The Bodley Head Monographs, London, 1960, p. 59.

Jörg Steiner: *The Bear Who Wanted to Stay a Bear* Illustrated by Jörg Müller. This translation by kind permission of Andersen Press Ltd.

Colin Thiele: *Blue Fin*, Weldon Publishing.

J. R. R. Tolkien: *The Hobbit*, © George Allen & Unwin, now Unwin Hyman, an imprint of HarperCollins Publishers Ltd (UK).

Cynthia Voigt: *Dicey's Song*, by permission of William Collins Sons & Company, now HarperCollins Publishers Ltd.

Jenny Wagner: *John Brown, Rose and the Midnight Cat* by Jenny Wagner, illustrated by Ron Brooks, published by Penguin Books Australia Ltd.

Sylvia Townsend Warner: *Letters*, published by Chatto and Windus, by permission of The Random Century Group Ltd.
Robert Westall: *The Scarecrows*, published by The Bodley Head, by permission of The Random Century Group Ltd.
Phyllis A. Whitney: *Writing Juvenile Stories and Novels*, reproduced by permission of the author.
Margaret Wild: *There's a Sea in My Bedroom*, published by Penguin Books Australia Ltd. *The Very Best of Friends* (illustrated by Julie Vivas) © 1989 Margaret Wild, published by Margaret Hamilton Books.

Every effort has been made to trace copyright holders, but in a few cases this has proved impossible. The publishers would be interested to hear from any copyright holders not here acknowledged.